# Essays and Studies 1989

# The English Association

The object of the English Association is to promote the knowledge and appreciation of English language and literature.

The Association pursues these aims by creating opportunities of co-operation among all those interested in English; by furthering the recognition of English as essential in education; by discussing methods of English teaching; by holding lectures, conferences, and other meetings; by publishing a journal, books, and leaflets; and by forming local branches overseas and at home.

## Publications

*The Year's Work in English Studies.* An annual bibliography. Published by John Murray (U.S.A.: Humanities Press).

*Essays and Studies.* An annual volume of essays by various scholars assembled by the collector covering usually a wide range of subjects and authors from the medieval to the modern. Published by John Murray (U.S.A.: Humanities Press).

*English.* The journal of the Association, *English* is published three times a year by the Oxford University Press.

*Newsletter.* A *Newsletter* is published three times a year giving information about forthcoming publications, conferences, and other matters of interest.

## Benefits of Membership

*Institutional Membership*

Full members receive copies of *The Year's Work in English Studies, Essays and Studies, English* (3 issues) and three *Newsletters*.

Ordinary Membership covers *English* (3 issues) and three *Newsletters*.

Schools Membership includes two copies of each issue of *English*, one copy of *Essays and Studies*, three *Newsletters*, and preferential booking and rates for various conferences held by the Association.

*Individual Membership*

Individuals take out Basic Membership, which entitles them to buy all regular publications of the English Association at a discounted price, and attend Association gatherings.

*For further details* write to The Secretary, The English Association,
The Vicarage, Priory Gardens, London W4 1TT.

# Essays and Studies 1989

*English economis'd:*
# English and British Higher Education in the Eighties

**Edited by**
**Martin Dodsworth**

**for the English Association**

JOHN MURRAY, LONDON
HUMANITIES PRESS,
ATLANTIC HIGHLANDS, N.J.

ESSAYS AND STUDIES 1989
IS VOLUME FORTY-TWO IN THE NEW SERIES
OF ESSAYS AND STUDIES COLLECTED ON BEHALF OF
THE ENGLISH ASSOCIATION

© The English Association 1989
First published 1989
by John Murray (Publishers) Ltd
50 Albemarle Street, London W1X 4BD

Typeset by Colset Private Limited, Singapore
Printed and bound in Great Britain by
Butler & Tanner Ltd, Frome and London

British Library Cataloguing in Publication Data

English economis'd: essays and studies 1989.– (Essays
and studies: v. 42).
1. Great Britain. Higher education institutions.
Curriculum subjects: English literature
I. Dodsworth, Martin   II. Series
820′.7′1141

ISBN 0-7195-4682-6

First published 1989 in the United States of America by
HUMANITIES PRESS INTERNATIONAL, INC.,
Atlantic Highlands, NJ 07716

The Library of Congress has cataloged this serial
publication as follows:

Essays and studies (London, England: 1950)
Essays and studies: being volume 42 of the new series of essays
and studies collected for the English Association. — 1950–
— London: J. Murray, [1950–

v.: ill.; 22 cm.

Annual.
Title varies slightly.
Vols. for 1950–1981 called also new ser., v. 3-v. 34.
Continues: English studies (London, England)

1. English literature—History and criticism.   2. English philology—Collections.
I. English Association.   II. Title.   III. Title: Essays & studies.
PR13.E4      820.4      36-8431
AACR 2 MARC-S

Library of Congress      [8509r85]rev5

ISBN 0-391-03659-9

# *Contents*

# Introduction

## MARTIN DODSWORTH

In the United Kingdom English as an academic subject has been 'economised'. Over the last ten years something like one in every six teachers of English in the universities has gone, not to be replaced. The situation is no better in the polytechnics and colleges which make up public sector higher education. There have, of course, been reductions in staffing in all academic subjects. English is a major subject of study at least in terms of the numbers of students it attracts; it has nevertheless suffered disproportionately in the current programme of economy. University historians, for example, have lost in the same period something like one in every eight of their number. It is symptomatic of the situation that these figures emerge from surveys conducted by voluntary organisations rather than from the Government or from the Universities Funding Council which oversees Government support for the universities.

Such 'economies' are not unique to Great Britain. If they were, this book would be of parochial interest only. But plenty of other western countries have known or can expect to know cutbacks of a similar kind. The essays gathered together in this volume reflect the response in one subject in the humanities to changes in financial (and moral) support for the higher education system, but also to a new call for accountability in a world where economic strategy has the upper hand. All teachers of English know this world and are implicated in it. That is why the responses outlined in this collection have a general interest for them.

Subjects like English, history and philosophy in particular have been charged with unproductive irrelevance to the economic struggle. Elitism is often added to irrelevance in the account of their wrongs. These charges constitute a pressure to change the nature of study in these subjects as great as that directly resulting from the withdrawal of funds. Reorganisation and rethinking are the order of the day; and the interest for a reader outside the United Kingdom will lie not only in what can be seen of resilience and resource in what follows, but in the extent to which the suggestions made, the tactics proposed, seem part of a process which higher education in general, in the western world at least, is undergoing.

1

Change in the subject is not the result of economic policy alone. British education as a whole is undergoing a transformation, and if that transformation is in part to do with adapting the system to the present needs of the economy, it is not entirely that. The essays in this book can only be properly understood if the scale of the changes in primary and secondary education now taking place alongside those in higher education is fully taken in. It seems, therefore, a good idea to begin by sketching a few of these changes as they affect English.

Change in the schools is already partly accomplished. In 1988 examinations for a single General Certificate of Secondary Education (GCSE) replaced a dual system in which sixteen-year-olds had opted to be examined either for the Certificate of Secondary Education or for the ordinary level of the General Certificate of Education. It was possible to be examined in some subjects for CSE and in others for GCE O level. The institution of a single level of examination may not sound stunning, but it is. In practice CSEs were regarded as inferior to O levels, though theoretically the two examinations were supposed to reflect a simple difference of approach. The choice between CSEs and O levels often implied, therefore, lower or higher expectations on the part of school or student. GCSEs, by setting one common examination, set one common level of achievement for schools and students alike. But there is more to it than that. GCSE examinations put great emphasis on coursework; the student is not judged on the basis of timed examination papers only. That means that the effectiveness of day-to-day teaching in the schools is more visible to examiners and a wider range of abilities in writing and reading is subject to scrutiny than in the old days. Teachers are more involved, too, in the business of examining, since they are responsible for the preliminary assessment of coursework. In English perhaps the greatest change has been to give a place in the syllabus to oral work. The ability to speak and listen well is no longer liable to be regarded as an optional extra.

The change to GCSE examinations has been largely successful, despite some poor and hasty organisation at the start. But it is far from the only change in secondary education. The Secretary of State for Education has decided to establish a National Curriculum for schools which will designate the amount of time to be given to different subjects and lay down standards of achievement whereby the performance of students and schools may be judged at virtually every point in a student's career from five to sixteen. These national criteria for assessment have been and remain a cause of anxiety for teachers both because they represent a considerable restriction on the freedom which they have known hitherto and because they multiply the opportunities for conflict between the individual's sense of what is good practice and the notion of it implicit in the national criteria. Teachers of English have more particular reasons for worrying that the utilitarian ethos of Government which lies behind these changes will be reflected in an emphasis on good spelling and some notionally 'correct' form of grammar at the expense of the child's imaginative development, traditionally the focus of English teaching in the schools. Early in 1987 a committee of inquiry into the teaching of English language was set up under the chairmanship of Sir John Kingman. It reported in 1988, recommending a 'model' of the English language as the basis for instruction in all schools. The report was accepted by Government, and its recommendations are by and large to be incorporated in those of the National Curriculum Working Group, which is chaired by Professor C. B. Cox. This Group has already made its recommendations on English for ages 5–11 and will report on ages 11–16 before the publication of this book. It strikes me as having steered its way very judiciously through the troubled waters of English studies, prescribing neither too much nor too little; however, its carefully unspecific recommendations on attainment targets for the various age-levels up to eleven proved unacceptable to the Minister, and teachers remain in suspense as to the practical implications for them of the National Curriculum. In particular, the extent to which literary studies will be incorporated into the secondary school curriculum remains unknown. Both the Kingman Report and the first part of Cox put emphasis on the importance of literary study, but it remains in doubt, given the Prime Minister's personal interest in old-fashioned grammar and her rumoured lack of interest in literature, whether this emphasis will be maintained. The matter is of concern to English teachers in higher education because of the possible effect on recruitment for English after age 16 and in the universities and polys.

In any case, there is more change as far as the 16–18 age-group is concerned. Compulsory education stops at sixteen; students going on to higher education, already possessed of certain basic requirements, study two or three subjects at the advanced level of GCE, or until recently have done so. Now, however, Government wants to widen education in the sixth form, partly, one suspects, in order to improve recruitment for higher-education science and technology. It recently commissioned yet another report, this time on the future of A levels. The Higginson Report recommended that students should, as a rule, take five subjects in the sixth form, mixing science and arts. Such mixing already takes place from time to time with A levels, but obviously five subjects give more opportunity for it than three. The Government, whilst accepting the principles underlying Higginson, chose not to take up his idea of scrapping A level in favour of a new kind of examination. Instead they have gone ahead with encouraging more students to take AS levels in addition to A levels. An AS level is supposed to be the equivalent of half an A level; the syllabus may be conceived of separately or as part of an existing A-level course. Schools have not been as enthusiastic as Government about AS levels, which may increase opportunity and widen the field of study for their pupils, but also complicate already complex timetables and make more work for a class of people who already feel themselves well taxed. Furthermore, although university vice-chancellors and principals have promised to accept AS levels as qualifying for university entrance, there is some doubt whether they are in practice welcome to the admissions tutors of Oxford and Cambridge. The result is a feeling that AS levels are not a good idea for high-flyers of any kind; this is likely to produce a down-grading of AS levels of the kind that took place with the CSE. But AS levels are enough of a problem for higher education English any way, because they require departments to be ready to admit students even less well prepared to study literature than in the past, yet students once admitted will be expected to qualify in the same short period of three years.

The point is not whether these changes are good or bad—for the record, I favour most, if not all, of them—but that they represent considerable stress for English teachers as a whole. There are not enough qualified teachers of English in the schools at present; goodness knows, therefore, how the increased demands of the National Curriculum, together with those for innovation in sixth-form teaching, are to be met, or what the effects of meeting those demands, in so far as they can be met, will be on recruitment for higher education. It is hard to believe that such reformist ferment, induced with a relative poverty of means and in haste, will be entirely satisfactory in the outcome.

Certainly, some of the emphases in the essays that follow should now be comprehensible. It is hardly surprising that Roger Sell, writing from the viewpoint of a European university, should stress the centrality of language to the study of English; that is perfectly in keeping with the old European philological tradition. It is not, however, consistent with English empiricism and its care for individual phenomena outside any systematic framework, a care which is part and parcel of that focus on the developing individual student by which Professor Sell attaches great store. It is therefore striking that Isobel Armstrong should also place language at the centre of attention, agreeing in this with Daniel Lamont. It is not the fact in itself—language, after all, was what both Richards and Leavis besought their students to attend to—so much as the way in which it is presented that is striking, for the proposal now is that language should be studied as a cultural practice. Instead of attending to language as the medium of literature, that is, the student of English will attend to literature as a specimen of language. Ronald Carter, in his essay, suggests something of what that is likely to entail. A renewed emphasis on language will transform English studies in British higher education and bring them much closer into line with what is to be found in departments of English on the Continent. At the same time it will adapt English studies to the requirements of the post-Kingman world, not merely by emphasising language-study, but also by producing syllabuses better suited to the more widely educated and less specialised student adumbrated in the Government's acceptance of Higginson's principles. Michael Irwin's reflections on inter-disciplinary study in the arts follow provocatively from this, for inter-disciplinary studies are also a means of offering the less specialised student the benefits, such as they are, of higher education in the arts. In their width of study and the opportunities they provide for new perspectives—provide teachers, at any rate—interdisciplinary studies are an attractive possibility for hard-pressed arts subjects like English. But they do press home rather more forcibly than before the question what arts degrees are *for*. The idea that a three-year course of study ought to have some coherence dies hard, for it is the specialisation that makes the relatively short time of study for the first degree possible. Abandon that idea, the idea of the unitary degree, and you move into an altogether different notion of what higher education in the arts should be like. Instead of the old-fashioned British three-year first-degree course, you find yourself approaching the four-year American model with its far wider range of choices, its relatively restricted attention to the individual and its distinctly preliminary quality as far as the more gifted student is concerned.

These essays show the way thinking about English in higher education is going. It is not the intention of the book to advocate a single position, though it is interesting that so much should centre on a renewed sense of the importance of English language. Personally, I

am sceptical about the ability to deliver a version of English studies in
the universities radically refocused in this way, though I concede that
the relatively recent development of English studies in the public
sector has produced something of the sort there. One reason for my
scepticism lies in the reduced numbers left to teach and administer in
university departments. Large-scale change is not easily thinkable in
prevailing conditions; the *appearance* of change is far more likely to be
what will emerge. An increase in inter-disciplinary studies, on the
other hand, by loosening up existing departmental structures could
produce the new emphasis by gradual means. This is likely to come
about, again as a consequence of Government intervention. For,
pursuing its policy of free-enterprise competitiveness, there are some
signs that the Government will encourage those universities that can
to take responsibility for fees and income into their own hands (at the
moment the Government has a large say in these matters). In effect,
the most successful universities would free themselves of Government
patronage. They would presumably continue with the old-fashioned
specialised degrees on which their success was founded. But where
would that leave the others? It would leave them certainly less able to
distinguish themselves from the polytechnics and colleges that make
up public sector higher education. Such a development would, I
think, tend to the erosion of the binary line as it is foreseen by Daniel
Lamont, and as far as the arts were concerned would lead to increased
emphasis on inter-disciplinary degrees, better suited as they are to the
enquiring but less certainly committed student.

It is noticeable how little of the changes which have taken place or
are anticipated have been initiated within higher education. Lyn
Pykett's essay concludes with a plea for greater involvement in schools
English on the part of higher education if an exclusively 'functionalist'
version of the subject is not to predominate in secondary education.
Although I do not take quite so dark a view of the changes taking
place, I do agree that they need to be more directly moderated by the
universities than has been the case. GCSEs and A levels are adminis-
tered by university-based groups like the London University Board of
Examinations, the JMB (Joint Matriculation Board), the SUJB
(Southern Universities Joint Board) and so on, but these generally
carry few members of university English departments, if any, and Lyn
Pykett is a rare example of someone within university English who
actually knows something of what is going on in schools. The reason
for this state of affairs is not hard to find; as the demand for university
productivity has increased, jobs that are not seen to be productive

(productive, that is, of publications or status, and preferably of both) have gone by the board. That is an effect of increased competitiveness, and must stand as sceptical footnote to the economic ethos. Economic considerations may nevertheless lead departments to involve themselves more in schools affairs as recruitment becomes more problematic: so much the better, though how it is to be done is not easy to see.

Isobel Armstrong's eloquent essay speaks of the intellectual pleasure at the heart of English studies, and I would endorse that quality. There are, however, some aspects of English studies noticeably unmentioned in any of these essays, and whose absence I find troubling. For example, the word *art* is missing, or at least has no prominence. I do not think that *creativity* figures here either. The word *moral* hardly leaps from the page. Yet indisputably poetry is an art, literature (a term to which I attach no exclusive power) has something to do with creative innovation, and the depiction of human life in literature insistently returns us to moral questions, even if criticism has not always wished to face up to them. These terms do not sum up all that there is to study in literature, and therefore in English, but they do say something about the satisfactions that continue to draw people of all kinds to read and re-read it. They are, certainly, difficult terms to use in relation to literary texts if we are trying to use them well; but they are among those that come readiest to hand when talking about books, whether the novels of Jane Austen or those of Philip K. Dick. My own belief is that the considerations which are implied by that readiness will ensure their continued currency in discussion of English writing; yet their obscurity in the debate conducted in this volume is cause for anxiety, a sign of how far the academic pursuit of English has become detached from the meaning found in it on the part of those on the outside of the subject *as* subject.

Peter Corbin's fascinating account of what English graduates actually do demonstrates the subject's viability as a way in to working life. It will be said that English cannot be considered to have trained all these students for the jobs they took, and that therefore they would have been better studying something more directly 'useful', something that *would* have trained them. Perhaps, however, their merit lay in their openness to suggestion, coupled with an ability to seize imaginatively the opportunities that that very openness brought with it. English students represent the possibility of change in patterns of employment, not an ossified system of specialised training for jobs which may have disappeared, in this fast-changing world,

by the time the training has been completed. They also represent, it
is to be hoped, a willingness to think in the human terms of a consciousness widened by literary and linguistic education: in terms of
a consciousness one might still dare to call, with whatever reserve,
imaginative. Economising English could be very bad for our imaginative health.

# English in Higher Education: 'Justifying' the Subject

## ISOBEL ARMSTRONG

It should not be necessary to 'justify' the study of English in the universities and polytechnics any more than the study of the humanities or social sciences. This needs to be said emphatically from the start. But given that one is embarking on an account of the importance of the subject at the present time, two questions are in order: to whom is this discussion addressed, and *what* is being described by the word 'English'? An answer to the second question will emerge here by tackling the first. I am writing with the educational policies of the present Government in mind, and that very large group of people who do not consider that higher education is particularly relevant to them, a group whom neither the Government nor the universities have seriously addressed. I am much less directly concerned with recent internal debates about what constitutes 'English'. There have been important challenges to the teaching of English which have come from within. The collection of essays edited by Peter Widdowson, *Re-Reading English* (1982), debated a 'crisis' which still requires serious thought, and some teachers of the subject believe that both 'English' and 'literature' are suspect categories of nineteenth-century bourgeois culture which are fundamentally disabling, so much so that the 'end' of English should be our aim. But such internal debates begin to look different if one starts with the assumption, as I do, that access to higher education has been disastrously restricted for too long, and that a huge expansion is necessary.

Higher education statistics are well known. Eight per cent of school leavers in this country go to universities, and only fourteen per cent of school leavers find their way to higher education, compared with twenty per cent in France, Germany and the Netherlands and forty-five per cent in the USA. One out of three sixteen-year-olds stays on at school, one out of five seventeen-year-olds stays on (the pool for higher education). In January of this year (1989) the Secretary of State for Education, in a surprising volte face, announced that he aimed for thirty per cent of school leavers, supplemented by mature students, women, and those belonging to minority ethnic groups in Britain, to be in higher education after the first decade of the next century, and declared that the increase had already begun (yes: but the small increase achieved for the academic year 1988–89 has been at the cost of larger classes in the polytechnics). It is important to take this ambition seriously if the future of English in the next two decades is to be thought out. For the moment it is necessary to put aside the blandness of these plans (for if this expansion is to be financed from private funds it will exclude from access precisely the groups intended to be enfranchised) and their apparent cynicism. The Secretary of State for Education, in spite of his new vision of an expanded higher education system, plans to admit untrained teachers into schools to meet the current shortage of teachers and has gone on record as saying that teachers do not need to know the history or theory of education in order to do their jobs well. However, it is necessary to consider the confusions which underlie these contradictions, for these do have a bearing on the way in which we think about our subject in the future.

This confusion might be addressed, in the first place, as the Samuel Smiles factor. A narrowly instrumental conflation of education and *individual* training and self-help runs deep in our society. Those in favour of more education often exploit the identification of education and training to claim that more advanced education means more money and a richer nation. 'Is it surprising that low skills and inadequate qualifications are two chief causes of our economic ills?' a *Guardian* leader recently asked in the course of an argument about expansion in higher education (January 30, 1989). Quite apart from the fact that this is effectively a covert argument about the need for more technologists and scientists rather than for general expansion, the argument about the need for skills is always, whether intentionally or not, an argument for *minimal* training. No one needs to be trained to perform a task or exercise a skill beyond what is required to complete it successfully. Thus Samuel Smiles argued, at a time when more sophisticated industrial needs in the mid-nineteenth century outstripped the nation's capacity to provide a workforce with skills, for a minimum of training (if any) and a maximum of individual effort.

> National progress is the sum of individual industry, energy, and uprightness, as national decay is of individual idleness, selfishness and vice. What we are accustomed to decry as great social evils, will, for the most part, be found to be but the outgrowth of man's own perverted life; and though we may endeavour to cut them down and extirpate them by means of Law, they will only spring up

again with fresh luxuriance in some other form, unless the conditions of personal life and character are radically improved.[1]

Many members of this Government have abandoned the grand aristocratic romanticism of Burke in favour of the petty romanticism of Smiles because it seems both democratic and energetic: all you need is the driving force to get on and your own manipulative efforts. The nostalgia of this atavistic primitivism leads to the assumption that teaching is a purely practical skill which has nothing to do with thought. It also leads to the belief that if we could only match training needs to market demand (as the new National Training Task Force set up to advise the Minister of Employment will attempt), whether it is the need for welders, information technologists, doctors or lawyers, we need only train the requisite minimum workforce for these tasks. Training is crucially important in a complex industrial society, but it is not education. It is in any case arguable that to respond to change and to new training needs (factors which this directorialist plan ignores) you *require* education, and that education is not a luxury item on top of training. But it is dangerous to justify education through training, because this way you always end up with it as an optional extra, something you can have if you are prepared to pay for it.

The Smiles factor influencing the Secretary of State for Education is in conflict with what might be called the Adam Smith factor, though this is a little unfair, since the present Government manifestly misreads Smith as it does not misread Smiles. The model of the firm, of producer and consumer (with its corollary of productive and unproductive industry) is now applied remorselessly to all forms of activity. Education is no exception to the metaphor of market forces and the Secretary of State's capacity to take the Government's metaphor for real has led to the understanding that if people want higher education enough they must have it. It has also led to the discovery that the arts side of education actually pays. The Policy Studies Institute found that the arts 'industry' employed 500,000 people and accounted for 1.2 per cent of gross domestic product in 1984. The *Guardian* compared the arts sector's contribution of £4 billion to overseas earnings with £3.8 billion from motor vehicles and parts, and suggested that a thriving arts base can generate industrial recovery. These figures are in happy consonance with the Government's metaphor, perhaps, but they are irrelevant to any real consideration of the way that metaphor works. Who is the consumer where education is concerned? Is it the student, who uses the services of the educator? Or is it the Government which, for the moment at least, pays for the bulk of higher education and might be said to use its products, the qualified students which emerge from it? Or is it the nation, whose taxes fund the education system? A quite different model of education emerges according to which of these elements you decide to designate as the consumer, but it is clear that any simple model of market forces breaks down.

Nevertheless the problems of the model have not prevented Mr Robert Jackson, the minister responsible for higher education, from playing with its application, clearly enjoying what he seems to hope will be a frisson of self-righteous horror experienced by academic purists. He sees 'academic lobbyists' on the analogy of monopolists—a kind of educational British Telecom—and vested interests campaigning for 'producer-defined specifications of what is necessary', such as the highest unit costs and the lowest staff/student ratio in the world, a higher proportion of GDP than Japan and most western European countries (*Times Literary Supplement*, December 30, 1988–January 5, 1989). At the same time as raising a serious question—how much should we spend on higher education?—he believes that individual groups of 'academic producers' should decide for themselves what to spend on particular subjects and that their policy should be dictated by consumer demand, or student demand, as it used to be called in the 1960s. He cannot resist enjoying the thought that his bracing language will produce 'ideological' arguments about the 'vulgarity' of consumer choice in higher education. Unfortunately Mr Jackson's language obscures the seriousness of the problems he raises: staff/student ratio and high unit costs came about from historical reasons; Britain produces uniquely a largely state-financed system of higher education, short in duration and high in quality, and the countries he compares it with do not. Do we want to go on like this or not? And in what way will the wider access envisaged by Mr Baker affect the argument? The matter of consumer choice is another question altogether.

If by consumer choice Mr Jackson means that active dialogue about the nature and content of knowledge which, long ago, in 1958, Raymond Williams called an 'amendment' created by the process of education itself, 'a society's confirmation of its common meanings, and of the human skills for their amendment', then few would challenge Mr Jackson's stress on the importance of enabling each new generation of students, each with new intellectual demands and needs, to participate in the reshaping of intellectual life.[2] But if this is what he means, the metaphors of consumerism and delivery are, not a matter of 'vulgarity', as he thinks and almost invites his proposals to be described, but just plain wrong. Vulgarity is merely his problem (he seems inordinately concerned with being described in this way), but the wrongness of the metaphor is ours. The wrongness of the metaphor is our concern because education is neither a skill, which has finite aims, nor a service, though it may provide both in the processes it initiates. The services of a dry cleaner, a caterer, a dentist, or a stockbroker, all these can be sold or provided, and all these can be dispensed with when the specific job they have done is completed. Varying degrees of optionality operate—you can put off having your clothes cleaned or even your teeth seen to, and you may be able to pay for a superior dry cleaner or dentist if you think it important to do so, or dispense with your stockbroker (witness the shake-out in the city after Black Monday). But you cannot sell thinking, or the capacity for analysis, whether of literature or physics, or that reflection into all forms of activity in a culture, which is what education initiates, in the same way. Moreover you cannot sell what is at the heart of education, shared and participatory activity, mutual and reciprocal learning, for without this interaction between teachers and taught, what Raymond Williams called the 'transforming energy' of intellectual life does not occur. The teacher cannot take away the pupil's mind to dry clean it (though perhaps the National Curriculum, depriving both teacher and pupil of academic freedom, has a go at this).

Of course, education, this interactive process which is neither a training nor a service, costs, and has to be costed. But this does not make it belong to market forces in the same way that the dry cleaner's services do. How to cost it involves fundamental ideological judgement. Where English studies are concerned that judgement is simply fudged if we consent to see them either in terms of their immediate instrumentality (some apologists take refuge in the notion of the 'transferable skills' of arts education) or in terms of objects of consumption. It may seem alarming to repudiate such thinking, for one may appear to be describing a singularly unnecessary and goal-less activity, an activity whose very end appears to *be* simply goal-lessness. Long ago J. S. Mill reflected on the unwillingness of either governments or individuals to enter into such useless and unproductive labour:

We know how easily the uselessness of almost every branch of knowledge may be proved to the complete satisfaction of those who do not possess it. How many, not altogether stupid men, think the scientific study of languages useless, think ancient literature useless, all erudition useless, logic and metaphysics useless, poetry and the fine arts idle and frivolous, political economy purely mischievous? Even history has been pronounced useless and mischievous by able men. Nothing but that acquaintance with external nature, empirically acquired, which serves directly for the production of objects necessary to existence or agreeable to the senses, would get its utility recognised if people had the least encouragement to disbelieve it.[3]

In an in many ways brilliant move, Matthew Arnold, who is important to us because his ideas became the founding principles of the academic study of English, seized upon this judgement and assented to it in a confoundingly paradoxical way which secured the future of English studies for nearly a century. Literary culture was to be paramount precisely because it was cut off from scientific and technological culture. It was concerned with permanent value, with the best that has been thought and said in the world, with maintaining tradition, with the ethical and the beautiful, with judgement and appreciation. It would replace religion in our society, becoming a consolation and stay. It says a great deal for Arnoldian thought that today people well-disposed towards intellectual life, often people well-disposed but not necessarily participating in it, assume that this is what literary study involves, and respect it. But however much can be taken from Arnoldian ideas (and more can be taken than hostile readers of Arnold believe) they will not do. They will not do particularly today.

An account of English studies which repudiates both narrow instrumentality and consumerism requires different and more robust principles. As historians have been willing to recognise more sharply than literary scholars, Arnoldian values belong to a historical and political situation quite different from ours, the crisis of reform in 1867 when the traditional ruling class sought new and more subtle ways of defining its powers. Richard Shannon, in *The Crisis of Imperialism 1865–1915*, writes:

As Arnold defined culture as the best that has been known and said transmitted from the past and thus made available by tradition, so 'right reason' was the historically conditioned intuition of the bearers of tradition in society, the ruling class. Arnold's defence of culture was, in political terms, the defence of an idea of a clerisy which had the capacity and the confidence and, most important of all, the legitimacy of traditionally derived right reason, to decide for society as a whole what is good and what is bad.[4]

It is arguable that Arnold certainly tamed ruling class values, that his post-Kantian understanding of aesthetic freedom was responsible for an educational system which has been, until recently at least, remarkably open, repudiating payment by results and a narrow account of education as the acquisition of facts. All this may be true, but it is not easy to democratise Arnoldian values, and if English studies are to survive as part of a common culture, they have to be democratised. For as soon as one begins to ask of the formulation, the best that has been thought and said, such questions as—*whose* best? *by* whom? and *for* whom? the best for which time? the best at which time? what constitutes the best? who decides?—the difficulties of sustaining the Arnoldian tradition become apparent. It is not necessary to repudiate the literature of the past but it *is* necessary to understand that what constitutes the material of literary study needs to be constantly added to and expanded. The materials of the past will always be the object of study, but we will ask different questions about them. A permanent ethical and aesthetic value does not reside inherently in literary works or objects of beauty, Kant said, but is *deemed* to belong to them by cultural consensus. Thus literary production—and cultural production generally—will not simply be revalued from time to time (like houses or antiques) but the nature of value itself, what it is and where it lies, is being continuously defined and redefined by negotiation and debate.

That this definition and redefinition, this negotiation, debate and dialogue, should be a communal matter, that it should be broadly based and command general participation, was understood by Raymond Williams when he wrote of the necessity for releasing in people the skills and energies to amend society's common meanings. Therefore, turning his back against the élitist pessimism which assumed an inevitable break between 'high' and 'low' culture (a definition which is a self-fulfilling prophecy) and refusing just as firmly the Gramscian Marxism which allocated a special place to the intellectual, he wrote of education as the means to create and perpetuate a common culture. He believed, writing in 1958, that unless this could be achieved the social fabric would be torn apart. Thirty years later, in the infinitely more complex and rapidly changing society of the 1980s, such views need reiterating and restating. Far from being less relevant today they are more relevant than ever. It is more necessary than ever, in a complex democratic society, that the largest possible body of people should benefit from and contribute to a process which liberates the energies of analysis and judgement, for as long as possible. This is not happening at the moment, and even the Government is beginning to show signs of alarm at the results, so it is in a mood of sombre realism that one turns to the specific place of English, and English in higher education, in the present situation.

English has always had a special place in academic study because it carries out its analyses with the same materials which are its objects of study—it is, as Shelley once said, both the materials of the sculpture and the tools which cut it—texts written in language analysed through language. For some people this has meant that its materials are so familiar that it is scarcely worth study, and for some this familiarity has guaranteed the centrality of the subject. Leavis, abusing the unique status of English, claimed that it subsumed all other subjects, but one does not have to make this unhelpful claim in order to understand its importance in the country where English is our 'native' language. Language, indeed, is at the heart of our subject, and one could say that the study of the literary text becomes an extension of the study of language. Nevertheless, if one asks what kinds of reflection English studies provide which other forms of study do not provide, or do not provide so fully, the answer is that it is reflection into language and reflection into the text.

To begin with language study, which now encompasses traditional philological and historical study, etymology and semantics, formal linguistics, semiotics and the study of the sign: all these forms of study teach something vital—that language changes. What we think of as the English language is a multiple language, still in flux, always renewing itself. Following from this, the second vital perception is that language is a cultural practice. Ferdinand de Saussure, so-called father of linguistics and modern language study, wrote of 'the importance of linguistics to general culture: in the lives of individuals and societies, speech is more important than anything else.'[5] For the study of language to remain solely the business of a handful of specialists, he said, would be a quite unacceptable state of affairs. In practice, the study of language is in some degree or other the concern of everyone. To be able to reflect into and develop the resources of language, to understand the history of the language and communications of the present, to recognise not only the ways in which they can be manipulated for ideological purposes, but also the ways in which one can oneself come into possession of linguistic creativity, is a prerequisite for dealing with the demands our media-laden and bureaucratic society makes on us.

It is important to see that this skill or practice does not merely provide language users with a sophisticated negative defence against the manipulation of power or a technique for efficient communication. Though it may well provide these things, they would not in themselves form the basis of a common culture. Only when each and every one of us are recognised as language-makers, actively participating in the making and amending of common meaning, can that come about. The belief that the uniformity of a so-called 'standard' language is an entitlement which will give everyone the same linguistic opportunities, whether they are white middle class, working class, black or Asian, thus ironing out class and racial difference, is, though sustained by the well-meaning Kingman report, fallacious. For one thing, differences are only concealed, not eradicated, when everyone speaks the same (witness the insipid 'democratic' neutrality of the average TV presenter's language): for another, an actual, definable, 'standard' language is a phantom; it does not exist except as a formal hypothesis. We can speak of precision in spoken and written language, of an understanding of structural complexity, of verbal expressiveness, of a subtle grasp of register, of insight into the nature of the multi-accentual sign, of critical awareness of meaning, all of which are necessary and desirable for the language-maker, and all of which demand considerable sophistication and an understanding of the history of meaning, of where words and ideas come from; but we speak at our peril of an abstract uniformity against which the language of individuals is measured. A glance at the history of the phrase 'standard language' reveals, as a colleague has recently shown, that those words themselves have changed radically over history; at one time they meant the language spoken in the public schools, whereas they now imply a level uniformity, as in a 'standard' nail, or plug.[6]

A genuinely enabling account of language, and one which makes the most rigorous and strenuous demands on teachers and taught, and which would enfranchise those groups whose first language is not English, is an account which understands language to be renewed every time anyone speaks or writes. Every individual is a practitioner who participates in the making of meaning and the *changing* of meaning, and every individual requires the skill, sophistication, critical awareness and confidence to achieve this. The corollary is that the history of language and cultural change needs to be more widely understood, for meaning and change of meaning is made through dialogue, debate and negotiation.

Aware of a history of silence and of being silenced experienced by women in our culture in particular, some feminist critics speak of the importance of freeing the oppressed or the silenced into language. But this idea requires extension: to be liberated into the resources of language, and in particular into an understanding of the multi-accentual sign, is everyone's need. Mrs Gaskell's novel, *Mary Barton*, contains an apposite parable about a breakdown of language. Wilson, an unemployed mill-worker who has been attending a dying man, goes to the house of the mill-owner, Carson, to obtain an infirmary order. He comes away with the wrong category of order and for a day so far ahead that it is useless, having been unable to explain the urgency of the case or to argue for an earlier order when he sees what decision Carson has taken. He has not been freed into language and fails, but, just as important, neither has the master, Carson. It is not a question of access to a 'standard' language (by London reckoning both would be speaking a Manchester dialect): it is that neither understands what language is *for*, so that one abuses power and the other is powerless. Neither man sees that unless they share a common capacity to use its resources, language can be used for the powerful and against the powerless. Today both Wilson and Carson would be negotiating with an array of doctors, hospital workers, consultants, counsellors, social workers, social security officers, insurance representatives, local government housing officers, gas and electricity firms, and possibly lawyers and tax men. To negotiate what is, after all, a matter of life and death, each and every one of these participants in crisis would need to be liberated into the resources of language. None of them would be merely manipulating the sign towards efficient communication: they would be participating, *self-consciously* and with full awareness of the possibilities of language, in a cultural practice. And here an understanding of what language is for does not simply make the negotiation of these complexities pleasanter or easier: it makes them possible.

Since the literary text is made of language, it seems logical to recognise its dependent position in the study of English, though not everyone might wish to agree to this. But this does draw attention to an understanding that needs to be much more widely disseminated in our culture than at present—to the textuality of the literary work, its nature as *representation*. The *constructed* nature of the text, its status as an artefact in language, makes it akin to other cultural documents, to political speeches, newspaper reports, scientific, historical and philosophical writing, letters, diaries, plays, films, videos. Rather

than trying to define a special place for the literary text, its affinity
with other cultural documents needs to be affirmed from the first, for
because it is a highly *visible* example of construction and representation, the sophisticated interpretative act required of its reader is fore-
grounded, and its self-consciousness transferred to less visible and
obvious forms of verbal or visual representation. For the fact that a
text is a representation makes the questions it represents no less
important. To relativise a text is not to negate the importance of its
propositions: it is simply to refuse to take them as absolute. The act of
*reading*, made as aware and alert as possible about the processes of
interpretation and transmission, is a crucial one for our society today.
Who made it? For whom? When? What is its place in history? How
does that define my history? How does my history define it? These are
essential questions in the interpretative process, essential because they
put one in possession of historical and ideological understanding and
the capacity for critique and investigation. This capacity for critique
and deconstruction is important only partly to form a protection
against government by advertising agency or business interests or the
nuclear lobby: it is important because it enables the capacity for widespread cultural debate. Such debate, such ability to be in control of
discussion and dialogue, is essential for the energies of a healthy,
participatory democratic society with complex issues to debate. This is
the way societies collectively create, share and renegotiate questions of
value. It is interesting in this respect that the Secretary of State for
Education has rejected any element of discussion of science and its
relation to value from the National Curriculum.

There are two other aspects of the literary text which mark it off
from an affinity with other cultural documents rather than affirm its
similarity to them, and these are equally important. The literary text,
having no immediate utility, is an experiment with the processes of
signification, with (often ambiguous) codes and signs and language,
an experiment in the making of meaning. It is a repository of cultural
and linguistic effort, where language is at its most subtle and demanding, not least because the text's language may have been determined
by accounts of linguistic function in the past which are now alien to us.
An analysis of language used in this way, and at this level of intensity,
is invaluable for that process of linguistic understanding and exploration to which I have already referred. But though it is an indispensable
support for this activity it also adds a new process to the act of learning
involved in English studies—the process of discovering intellectual
pleasure. Intellectual pleasure, in particular the shared pleasure of

teacher and learner in the process of discovery which comes about through the close analysis of the language of a text, a pleasure derived from mutual labour, is, I have found, an almost inevitable result of work on a text in class. Its importance cannot be overestimated. Intellectual pleasure, recognised even by such relatively conservative educationalists as Locke, pleasure, as opposed to recreation, is deeply energising and motivating, and within the reach of us all, because work on a text can be conducted in so many ways and in so many registers.

Pleasure has not been much reckoned with recently, perhaps because we have not developed a vocabulary which can describe it. It is seen to belong to the private sphere and not to the public and social domain, as I believe it does. It is related to another capacity called forth by the literary text, which is also undervalued and also mistakenly believed to belong to the inner, private life, and that is the capacity for imaginative activity. The fictions of the literary text, even those produced in the present, are conjured by language which requires a critical, imaginative and analytical effort of assimilation and interpretation if they are to be fully understood. Paradoxically, writing of the past which is now no longer generally read or whose language is not immediately accessible, often once popular texts, require an even greater effort of imagination and analytical and historical intelligence than the familiar 'classics' seem to demand. The act of imagination in this context is not a private, self-expressive act. It is a public and social commitment to knowledge and cultural understanding because language falls into the public sphere and because the imagination and empathy is organised, intellectually shaped and directed, controlled and extended by the desire for analysis and the desire for understanding of the unlike experience, the things we cannot know except through the discipline of the imagination. One's defence of imaginative activity would resemble the same case for 'empathy' history: in both cases the mistake made by its opponents has been to assume that the act of imagination implies total identification of the present and the past instead of the attempt to understand difference.

What would the syllabus and curricula for English studies in higher education look like as a consequence of the emphasis on language for a common culture and an account of the literary text as representation? Space allows me the most abbreviated of descriptions, but it is possible to give a general indication of the directions we might go in. We would do all that we do now, and encourage the variety which has always characterised our higher education system. But to foster language awareness we would make sure that students took possession of the history of language, both as the history of its structure and formation and, crucially, as the history of language and cultural change, the history of the way language has been conceptualised at different points in our culture, the politics of language: we would make sure that they were introduced to speculative and theoretical accounts of language, and understood where conflicting accounts of language come from through an understanding of the history and theory of communication: we would make sure that they can research into the nature of the multi-accentual sign in our culture and that they discover the ways in which groups, sub-groups, minorities (for instance, ethnic minorities, women) have negotiated linguistic problems. Above all, since language is a cultural practice, students would be practitioners across a wide variety of forms. Just as music students compose in order to understand musical form, creative writing, the composition of rhetoric and metaphor, pastiche, commentary, debate, a variety of dealings with the sign, verbal, aural and visual, would add to the student's work with the formal analysis of the essay. People come into language by using it.

Much of such study would overlap with the study of the literary text, because we would extend what we understand by the text. In my view written texts would still form the core of English studies, though English studies and cultural studies involving the analysis of a wide range of artefacts are not incompatible with one another, as so many people seem to think. A history of the way texts have been read, their place in culture, and the ideological problems they raise, the retrieval of texts forgotten by history (for instance, writings by women, working class writers, ethnic sub-groups, or uncanonised popular texts) studied concurrently with those questions of theory and form which aesthetic objects and fictional constructions generate by their nature as representation, are at the heart of our discipline. A first-hand imaginative and analytical response to textual materials is a prerequisite for dealing with these questions. People come into imagination and thought by imagining and thinking.

To end as I began, it is not necessary to 'justify' our subject, though it could be said that it is useful to consider how English studies can be 'justified', in the sense of being adapted and changed, as circumstances change. Always an interdisciplinary subject, it will be more so in the future. What I have said is abbreviated, and, rather than being new, is intended as a challenge to those frivolous aspects of current thinking which consider education in the name of instrumentality or consumerism. What I have said presupposes that, from the youngest primary child to the senior researcher, the study of English is a matter of making and remaking language and cultural meaning. My argument also presupposes that far more people than are at present allowed to benefit from it are capable of the intellectual and imaginative inventiveness which the study of English in higher education can develop. I do not claim exclusive rights for my subject (in fact, a mixed Arts and Sciences first year in the degree course would be worth trying for), but simply describe what is important about it.

Of course, in repudiating narrow instrumentality, I do not repudiate the 'uses' of English. Just as road, rail and communications networks both create and perpetuate the infrastructure which sustains the complex life of an advanced industrial country, English is one of those disciplines which help to create the cultural infrastructure of a complex community. We have all seen the horrifying results which occur when the material infrastructure is allowed to decay. The results of allowing the cultural infrastructure to decay could be, and in many ways are becoming, just as horrifying, as people drop out of the participatory project of making common meaning or are excluded from it. The results of enabling many people to be language-makers, and of enabling many people to have access to the discipline of the imagination, are unpredictable, and almost certainly make governments uncomfortable in the short term. But it would be no exaggeration to say that it was general access to the imagination which was responsible for the abolition of slavery, and which has been responsible in our own day for the pressure which has allowed Green issues (only a few years ago regarded as the theme of crazy conservationists) to come on to the agenda, or which has allowed the debate about rape to become a central issue, not only in feminist thinking, but more generally in our society. No one can predict how new cultural meanings will be made by the educated analytical imagination, or what they will be. But this is precisely why we should educate for that adaptability, flexibility and inventiveness which enable common meanings, and new meanings, to come into being.

The ultimate cost of blocking the energies which expand cultural possibility could be immense, and there are signs, after a decade of decline and contraction in higher education (not to speak of degradation elsewhere in the education system), that those blocked energies are already doing some damage. We have taken so many huge steps backwards in the last decade that it seems incredible that what J. S. Mill, hardly a revolutionary figure, was saying over a hundred years ago has to be restated as if it were new:

> If we ask ourselves on what causes and conditions good government in all its senses, from the humblest to the most exalted, depends, we find that the principal of them, the one which transcends all others, is the qualities of the human beings composing the society over which the government is exercised . . . Whenever the general disposition of the people is such that each individual regards those only of his interests which are selfish, and does not dwell on, or concern himself for, his share of the general interest, in such a state of things good government is impossible.[7]

The current concern with 'Victorian' values, recently described by Gertrude Himmelfarb, in a strangely ahistorical pamphlet for the Centre for Policy Studies, as 'hard work, sobriety, frugality, foresight', democratic values requiring no special talent or gifts and locating responsibility within each individual, forgets that other Victorians, even those brought up in the tradition of individualism to which these Samuel Smiles values belong, struggled to think of what Mill called the 'general good'.[8] A literary, a critical imagination, would have shown Gertrude Himmelfarb that other Victorians, Mrs Gaskell, for instance, placed their hope in the values of community and mutual support which they saw as the virtues of the poor. Education for the intricate society of the twentieth and twenty-first centuries, in a truly participatory democracy, will surely offer a wider vision than that proposed by the nostalgia for a Victorian society that never was. English studies, providing the basis of a common culture through their capacity to free people into language, will certainly play a part in creating and sustaining the wider vision our society needs.

## Notes

[1] Samuel Smiles, *Self-Help; With Illustrations of Conduct and Perseverance*, London: John Murray, 1905, p. 3.

[2] Raymond Williams, *Resources of Hope*, London: Verso, 1989; from *The Guardian*, 3 February 1989, p. 23.

[3] John Stuart Mill, 'Representative Government', *Utilitarianism, Liberty, Representative Government*, ed. H. B. Acton, London: J. M. Dent, 1972, p. 254.

[4] Richard Shannon, *The Crisis of Imperialism 1865–1915*, London: Paladin Books (Collins), 1976, p. 34.

[5] Ferdinand de Saussure, *Course in General Linguistics*, ed. Jonathan Culler, revised edition, London: Peter Owen, 1974, p. 7.

[6] Tony Crowley, 'Language in History: "That Fair Field" ', forthcoming in *News from Nowhere*.

[7] Mill, p. 192.

[8] Gertrude Himmelfarb, 'Victorian Values and Twentieth-century Condescension', London: Centre for Policy Studies, 1987.

# Beyond A-level English: English in the sixth form and universities

## LYN PYKETT

The conclusion is inevitable that the curriculum of the Sixth Form cannot be drawn up with the needs of only future university students in mind. . . . it seems that on educational grounds we shall need a much greater elasticity in the shape of sixth form courses.

Crowther Report 1959, p. 265

On nearly all of the major issues a remarkable consensus emerged from the evidence. One of these was the need for the sixth form years to provide a broad and valuable experience. Since A levels took the place of Higher School Certificate they have assumed a wider role than the preparation for higher education which they played almost exclusively in their earlier years.

Higginson Report, 1988, pp. 1–2

The rather tattered view of literary studies as the common pursuit of true judgement is nowhere more undermined than in the recent and current history of the relationship between English as a school subject and English in the universities. If one is to judge from 'in-house' professional journals such as *The Use of English* and *English in Education*, or indeed much of the literature on the teaching of English 16–19, school teachers and university lecturers regard each other's work—if they regard each other at all—with mutual incomprehension (sometimes amounting to wilful misprision), distrust, hostility, and even, occasionally, contempt.

Public examinations, the bane of English literature teaching since its inception as a school and university subject, have provided a focus for much of the dissension and debate, but the issues are wider and deeper. They relate, on the one hand, to a growing factionalism within English studies, a contest about the definition of the subject which is, in part, an internal professional and ideological battle, but which is also connected to broader developments in the culture at large. On the other hand, the cultural revolution, or more correctly philistine counter-revolution of 'Thatcherism' has threatened to precipitate a crisis in English studies, and has certainly played an increasingly important part in shaping the agenda of the debates about the nature and function of English within the school curriculum. It is in these contexts that I want to examine the present state of English 16–19, and its perceived relationship to the demands of the universities, to speculate on possible future developments in the 16–19 curriculum, and to assess some of their implications for university schools of English.

Traditionally, as far as the universities have been concerned, English 16–19 has meant A-level English literature taken in the sixth form. However, since the 1960s students staying in full-time education after 16 have been able to choose from a growing range of post-16 courses in 'English' in a number of different kinds of institutional settings. Students at 18 + now enter universities and polytechnics from sixth-form colleges, colleges of further education, and tertiary colleges, as well as from the school sixth form. However, A-level English literature is still the usual direct route to a degree course in English.

It seems to be a truth universally acknowledged that teachers of A-level English, like their colleagues in other disciplines, feel confined by the straitjacket of the demands of the A-level syllabus and its dominant forms of assessment. In the case of English literature the straitjacket takes the form of a course of prescribed texts, assessed by means of a final timed examination requiring essays on the set texts and (for most boards) on unseen extracts from other literary works. Except for Alternative syllabuses, which I shall discuss later, both syllabus and examination are externally set. All are designed to test:

1. *Knowledge*—of the content of the books studied and where appropriate of the personal and historical circumstances in which they were written;
2. *Understanding*—extending from simple factual comprehension to a broader conception of the nature and significance of literary texts;
3. *Analysis*—the ability to recognise and describe literary effects and to comment precisely on the use of language;
4. *Judgement*—the capacity to make judgements of value based on close reading;
5. *Sense of the past and tradition*—the ability to see a literary work in its historical context as well as that of the present day;
6. *Expression*—the ability to write organised and cogent essays on literary subjects[1]

As early as 1918, when the 18 + examination was established, the English Association declared its disapproval of 'purely external examination in English literature, in which there is no direct contact between the Examiner and the teacher', on the grounds that 'the style of question set determines the method of teaching', and thus external examining boards 'usurp functions which properly belong to the school' (quoted in Newbolt, p. 303). In 1979 the Schools Council English 16–19 Project reported widespread dissatisfaction with the externally set, timed examination which requires the student to write on three, four or five major works of literature in three hours or less. John Dixon has outlined some of the difficulties and constraints of the external examination:

> The examiner must try to find the one or perhaps two questions on each text that will stimulate the majority of candidates, not reward them for second-hand opinions, not demand too detailed a recall of the text, and not require more than thirty to sixty minutes for a reasonable answer . . . these conditions are precisely the opposite to those the same examiners, as teachers of literature, would normally want to encourage 16-to 19-year-olds to work in (Dixon, p. 14).

Rightly or wrongly, teachers of A-level English attribute the forging of their manacles to the universities. The recent Higginson Report adds its voice to the clamour of dissatisfaction with the 'unnecessary dominance of university needs in the determination of A-level objectives' (para 4.4). It is certainly true that universities exert a strong downward pressure on A-level syllabuses, and teaching practices. However, they do so perhaps as much through teachers' perceptions and expectations as through any clearly formulated demands of their own. This is partly a matter of the perceived professional status of university departments which 'occupy positions of high prestige in the social structure of the discipline', and are thus able to 'perpetuate attitudes which are not or have ceased to be relevant to the nature of the subjects they teach' (Reid, p. 61). However, the most malign aspect of the 'unnecessary dominance of university needs' is their use of A level as the key instrument in their admissions procedures. Peter Hollindale expresses a widely held view when he deplores the constraints imposed on the pattern of sixth-form teaching and on the shape of the sixth-form curriculum by the use of A level 'for extraneous purposes, above all in serving as a visa for entry into further and higher education' (p. 30). The disproportionate influence of university demands on A-level English are put into perspective when one notes that only a minority of A-level students of English seek admission to higher education at all, and, despite its continuing popularity as a first degree subject, only a minority of that minority intend to study English.

One cannot deny that university English departments, like those in many high-demand subjects, have evolved their selection criteria, with their emphasis on high performances in A level, fairly unreflectingly, and until very recently have applied them in a cavalier fashion. However, despite their heavy reliance on high A-level grades, especially in English literature, university lecturers in English are just as likely as their schoolteacher colleagues to admit that they are neither a wholly reliable indicator of future performance, nor necessarily the most suitable preparation for further study in English in higher education. Many teachers in both sectors deplore the kinds of reader and reading produced by the 'laborious boredom of set book study' (Hollindale, p. 30), and the 'microscopic concentration on a very narrow range of texts' (Peter Daw, p. 65) required or encouraged by so many A-level syllabuses. University lecturers in particular are likely to lament the A-level student's lack of historical sense. Some lecturers may express this in terms of ignorance of 'the tradition', others as ignorance of the social and historical conditions of production of literary works, but both groups are exercised by the student's lack of a sense of the history of forms and genres, which persists despite the examining boards' general commitment to developing a 'sense of the past and tradition', (fifth in the list of skills tested, quoted earlier), and JMB's specific aim to present the subject as a discipline that is *inter alia* 'historical (setting literary works in the context of their age)'. Recently these longstanding discontents with the 'obstructions' (Hollindale) of A-level teaching have been voiced with a new and growing urgency by teachers in public sector schools and colleges. Many sixth-form teachers, for a variety of reasons, have been led to ask, as do John Brown and Terry Gifford in a recent essay on 'creative responses in the sixth form', why 'as the summit of English Studies in schools . . . is A-level English often so disappointing?' (in Lee, p. 370).

One answer to this question must surely be that the core of the traditional A-level syllabus has changed remarkably little in the last twenty years. There have, of course, been a number of developments during the last decade, such as the proliferation of Alternative syllabuses to which I shall return shortly. Other imaginative innovations by individual boards include JMB's 'English World Wide' option, the period papers offered by the Cambridge Board and in the 'extended reading' component of the Oxford syllabus, and the London Board's 'Topics in Literature' option. Nevertheless, I have been struck by just how easy it is to reconstruct, from the central syllabus of each of the A-level boards, almost exactly the same course (even the same texts) which I and my contemporaries followed in the early 1960s: Shakespeare, Chaucer, Milton, Jane Austen, Hardy.

The survival power of the traditional A level is all the more remark-able when one considers the scale of the changes in the nature and social composition of 'the sixth form', following the raising of the school-leaving age, the advent of comprehensive schools and mixed-ability teaching, and the large increase in the numbers of pupils staying on in post-16 education. There has also been a great increase in the numbers of pupils taking A levels. In 1951 37,000 candidates presented themselves for 104,000 subject entries at A level, by 1985 there were 380,000 candidates and 635,000 subject entries; in 1985 A-level English was taken by 59,483 candidates—17,738 boys and 41,745 girls.[2]

A great variety of teaching practices, and a number of different definitions of the subject have been produced in response both to the changes in the structure and composition of schools and colleges, and changes in the wider culture. 'English' in the primary schools and in the earlier stages of the secondary school curriculum has been trans-formed by child-centred approaches to learning, by the increased emphasis on children's own language and on their experience of their own immediate culture, and by a growing interest in children's creativity. Throughout the 1960s and 1970s both the form and the content of English teaching have changed as the boundaries of the subject have been extended and opened up to an increasing range of approaches. The 'Growth through English' movement, Basil Bernstein's work on the language of working-class children, and M. A. K. Halliday's advocacy of 'productive' language teaching, based on his work on language acquisition and development[3] are just some of the elements involved in this transformation of the subject, and the redefinition of its aims and methods.

In what now seems to have been the brief flowering of egalitarianism and social justice of the post-war period, English teach-ers and educational theorists began to concern themselves more and more with the curriculum needs of the majority of pupils, rather than the academic minority. In 1963 the Newsom Report affirmed that 'the overriding aim of English teaching must be the personal development

and social competence of the pupil' (p. 153). One of the chief consequences of these developments was a change in the place and role
assigned to literature teaching. As Margaret Mathieson points out,
although the Newsom Committee among others supported 'the continued teaching of literature and discrimination', others, most notably
the New Left, deemed ' "Great literature" ... inappropriate and
inaccessible to the majority of our pupils whose time should first be
spent on extension of their linguistic competence; its inclusion in all
pupils' curricula, with the inevitable exclusion of working-class culture, implicitly supports the present social structure with all its
inequalities' (p. 140).

There have been many gains from these redefinitions of English.
My own experience of teaching undergraduates in English suggests
that they are now more used to discussing their ideas, and more
willing to do so, than they were fifteen years ago. This improved
oracy, however, has been accompanied in some cases by a decline in
writing skills. Moreover, it is by no means self-evident, nor easily
demonstrable that the working-class children whose needs many of the
new strategies were primarily designed to meet have benefited from
them universally and unproblematically. The danger of some of these
approaches is that they can leave children exactly where they started,
lacking the linguistic tools and cultural perspectives which might
empower them to take control of and transform their situation. The
belief of James Britton, John Dixon and others that 'children will
arrive at maturity by their own efforts, creating an adequate world-
picture out of the material that comes their way by active talk and
writing' (Allen p. 67) has sometimes led to the teacher's abdication of
responsibility for teaching. In their most extreme forms some of the
child-centred pedagogies, despite their admirable egalitarian objectives, have resulted in what can appear to be a bloody-minded refusal
by English teachers to share their linguistic powers and more varied
cultural experience with their pupils; in short, a refusal to share the
cultural capital they have themselves acquired.

Another consequence of the redefinition of the subject, and the
proliferation of approaches to its teaching has been an increasing
factionalism within the profession. As David Allen has noted, 'It has
been characteristic of recent years . . . for English teaching to be seen
as a series of opposing choices—*either* knowledge *or* response, *either*
discipline *or* enjoyment, *either* subject *or* individuality . . . In particular,
the stress on the learning individual has been seen as excluding the
claims of the subject [English], or tradition, or a culture' (p. 105).

Whatever the merits or problems, the changing nature of English from 5 to 16 has in turn exerted pressure on the shape of the post-16 curriculum. In addition, the open or at least greatly increased access to 'sixth-form' education has also led to changed perceptions of what is needed by, and is indeed accessible to, the 16–19 group. As W. A. Reid predicted in 1972, the comprehensive sixth form has tended to 'break up the present relatively stable pattern of beliefs about sixth-form education' (p. 105).

These changes have produced an ever-increasing sense of disjunction between the various versions of 'English' offered in schools and colleges, and between the various levels of English provision in secondary and higher education. This disjunction may be examined from two points of view: the experiential and the institutional. On the one hand there is the disjunction experienced by students and teachers as they move from work at one level to another; on the other there is the disjunction in the way the subject is constituted and defined at various levels in the curriculum.

The Higginson Report voices a common critique of the A-level system when it endorses the view of an anonymous respondent that, 'the most fundamental error in the traditional GCE system was that each stage was designed to be suited for those who were going on to the next. Schoolchildren who were not good enough to go on were regarded as expendable' (p. 2). While many fifth- and sixth-year teachers will be able to people the history of waste which the last sentence implies, many will also recognise that the present two-tier GCE system (now GCSE/GCE) is not particularly efficient in delivering the results suggested by the first sentence. Robert Protherough's work on the Hull Students of English Project[4] suggests that students, and possibly also their teachers, find that no stage of secondary English teaching prepares adequately for the next. For example, 25 per cent of Protherough's survey group felt that English at 16 + (usually O Level) had left them unprepared for the greater range of reading required by A level, while precisely the same criticism was made of A-level courses by 50 per cent of those on degree courses in English. Similarly, both A-level and university students felt unprepared by the previous stage of their English studies for the greater independence of thought and level of critical analysis required by the next stage. This experiential disjunction is likely to become more pronounced following the apparently successful introduction of GCSE, with its emphasis on coursework, student-centred learning, personal response, and varied forms of writing. Most A-level boards have in fact already modified their syllabuses for 1990 in the light of developments at GCSE and AS level, and many plan further revisions.

The disjunction in the way in which English is constituted as a discipline is perhaps seen most clearly at the point where English literature becomes separated from 'English'. For some, this break occurs from 14 to 16 in the preparation for the 16 + literature examination (now, most commonly, GCSE). Until very recently the most radical break has been that which occurs after the fifth form, when, as Douglas Barnes has noted, 'for the majority literature disappears from the syllabus, [and] for the minority who are to go on to study English for A level, literature becomes the whole of their English study' (p. 259).

Many of the dissatisfactions with traditional A-level syllabuses, and certainly much of the public polemic amongst professionals focuses precisely on that term 'literature', on what it includes, and more problematically, on what it excludes. At A level, 'literature' most frequently includes the major fictional and imaginative works of great writers, but excludes much that has been included earlier in the curriculum—other forms of written discourse, especially popular forms, not to mention visual forms such as film and television. Equally problematic is the disjunction between the variety of writing practices and forms encouraged in the earlier stages of the curriculum, and the analytic critical discourse, 'the narrow specialisations of critical appreciation and the "scholarly" essay' (Spicer, p. 20), the 'polished, complete piece of literary criticism' (Daw, p. 66) felt to be required by A level.

Although sixth-form teachers and university lecturers frequently profess their dissatisfaction with traditional A-level courses and the kind of reader and writer they produce, in practice both groups have been rather slow to respond to the fact that there is quite literally an alternative in the now well-established and proliferating Alternative syllabuses offered by most of the A-level boards, and more recently, in a number of innovative A-level courses in English Language, and A- and AS-level courses in English (combined language and literature).

A-level courses in English Language are now offered by JMB, London and SUJB. These courses aim, as the JMB syllabus puts it, 'to combine learning about the nature and functions of language in human thought and communication with learning how to use English more effectively' (JMB Revised Syllabuses 1989). JMB requires a theoretical knowledge about language and society, language acquisition, varieties of language and language change, as well as requiring students to explore and use a variety of communicative forms in a range of media. The London syllabus is similarly eclectic, and although it emphasises 'empirical investigation of English in use, both written and spoken' (London Syllabus, June 1990/Jan 1991) it also requires theoretical and historical knowledge. A critical investigation of 'the use of language for a variety of purposes' (JMB English Syllabus, 1989) forms the central aim of the combined language and literature courses offered at A level by AEB and London, and at AS level by AEB, JMB and London. All of these courses encourage a critical awareness of a wide range of language uses in a variety of media, and all place great emphasis on developing the student's own writing abilities.

Alternative English syllabuses were developed in the 1970s in an attempt to connect the teacher, the pupil, and the kinds of work done in the classroom more directly to the examiner and the examination process. The additional syllabus devised by the AEB in 1976 was perhaps the most wide-ranging of the early developments. The aims and objectives of the proposed syllabus were (*inter alia*):

> to extend the range of English studies in the sixth form and, whilst retaining the traditional critical essay on a set text, to give the opportunity for more varied work; to widen the reading of A-level students beyond a limited number of set texts;
> to enable the student to pursue in greater depth a particular interest in literature, whilst ensuring that he [*sic*] also reads major writers' work;
> to give the student an opportunity to work under conditions which scholars would regard as essential, i.e. with access to texts and reference works and without a time-limit of forty-five minutes or an hour for a unit of work;
> to provide an opportunity for the teacher to participate in the assessment of students' work . . .;
> to obtain and assess a wider and more varied sample of the student's work in English;
> to maintain comparability with other A-level syllabuses by allocating the majority of marks to an externally set and marked examination but at the same time to provide an opportunity for individual choice in a substantial part of the syllabus (Dixon, p. 67).

These broad aims and objectives have been adopted in a variety of different forms by several boards. There are now a number of Alternative syllabuses which encourage a degree of movement away from prescribed-book study, and an exclusive concentration on the major works of 'great' writers. In some cases groups or individuals may, within certain constraints, construct their own syllabus; many Alternatives encourage extended reading; open book examinations (some boards even allow students to use their own self-annotated texts) are used to develop different ways of reading from those produced in candidates whose destination is the four-question, timed, bookless examination.

However, most *aficionados* of Alternative syllabuses reserve their greatest praise for the coursework element which enables both teachers and pupils to develop organically from their earlier experience of a more broadly defined English. Reporting on the Cambridge Alternative syllabus (formerly 9001) Peter Daw notes that 'the evidence for real engagement with the text is so much clearer in . . . coursework essays than in . . . examination scripts [which] . . . reveal haste, memorised quotations from texts and critics strung loosely together in an often valiant attempt to make them relevant to the question set, while showing little evidence of anything approaching literary response, sincere enjoyment, or individual thought' (p. 63). The coursework folder usually requires students to engage in an extended piece of writing, and encourages them to produce a variety of written forms, for example, diaries, journalism, and creative responses such as parody or the continuation of 'missing scenes' of works studied.

We know that the recently introduced AS levels have not, so far at least, attracted either a large number or a wide range of candidates. The Government intends that 95 per cent of all schools and colleges offering A levels will provide at least two AS-level courses by 1990. However, in 1988 only one in 25 sixth-formers was involved in AS-level courses, and over 90 per cent of these were taking only one subject at this level. AS-level courses were offered in 2800 schools and colleges (i.e. approximately one in seven), with former grammar schools, now largely in the independent sector, the keenest providers. General Studies (1782 candidates), Maths (818), and Computing (658) were the most popular options, followed by English (411) and French (383)[5].

It would be interesting to have statistics for the take-up rate of Alternative A-level syllabuses. As recently as 1986 Peter Daw, an enthusiastic supporter, lamented the fact that their existence seemed to have escaped the notice of a large number of English teachers. There is, however, already a well-documented literature on the ways in which particular Alternative syllabuses work in practice. These case histories usually emphasise the liberating aspects of such courses for both teachers and pupils. Andrew Spicer, for example has welcomed the 'more flexible approach to what constitutes acceptable texts and ways of reading and writing about them' (p. 187) provided by AEB 660. Margaret Peacock and Elaine Scarrat have described how their own version of this syllabus has enabled them to build upon changes in lower school English which take account of the cultural diversity of the pupils of their London comprehensive, and to develop an A-level course which fosters 'an active investigation of what literature is rather than a passive appreciation of "great" works' (p. 105).

Some critics of A-level English, however, dismiss Alternative syllabuses as 'flawed and devitalised because of their failure to break with the models of English studies represented in conventional syllabuses'. The new A levels, according to Roy Goddard's blistering critique, are 'rooted in the assumptions, the perspectives and the practices of the old A levels', which were and are designed to cream off those students who can internalise and reproduce the definitions of literature and the ways of reading 'that predominate in university English departments' (p. 13). Although this position is untypical of English teachers at large, its underlying premise is widely shared; that the educational efficacy (variously defined) of A-level English is seriously distorted by its primary aim of preparing students for higher education, and in particular of producing undergraduates for university departments of English. These latter are regarded by teachers either as the noble guardians of the national literary heritage, the preservers of an endangered high culture which has retreated into the ivory towers to escape the onslaughts of a voracious mass culture, or as a closed shop or freemasonry, bent on defending the indefensible élite of the dead, difficult and largely unread.

It would seem that numerous strands of the critique of A-level English, and of the limitations of the 16–19 curriculum coalesce in their perceived relationship to the arcane practices of the universities, and their restrictive and élitist definitions of literature. It would be foolish to claim that university departments of English *en bloc* are in the vanguard of a radical redefinition of English studies, but it is equally foolish to argue that they are merely bastions of reaction. Few English departments in British universities now perpetuate the unproblematic version of hegemonic English studies so frequently set up as a straw target by would-be reformers of A level. The canon, the monolithic literary heritage against which Goddard and others rail, and in opposition to which they habitually define their alternative projects has, at least in theory, been dismantled, and reassembled or dispersed according to the critical positions adopted by particular practitioners. However, it should be said that the course content and structure endorsed by institutions often lags behind the critical positions held by the groups of individuals who teach in them.

Certainly university English departments have little room for complacency. There is still much they could do in response to both the changing definitions of the subject implied by the challenges of recent literary theory, and the changes in the schools and colleges. Their role should not be blindly and uncritically to follow 'consumer-demand'[6] but in the interest of the subject and its general educational objectives, as well as in the interests of greater social justice and cultural vitality[7] university English departments should inform themselves of the developing situation in the schools, and work collaboratively with the best practice. For example, university lecturers in English could play a much greater role than they presently do in involving themselves in discussions about and implementation of curriculum changes at A level.

Much important work remains to be done in rethinking teaching methods and the shape and content of university courses in the light of the changes that have occurred in the schools over the last twenty years. GCSE, the National Curriculum, attainment targets, the Technical and Vocational Education Initiative (TVEI) will all bring further fundamental changes in the secondary curriculum. Despite its initial snub to the Higginson Report the Government is committed to the broader sixth-form curriculum advocated by both the Higginson Committee and the Council for Industry and Higher Education (which includes leading industrialists and university vice-chancellors). In his speech to the Committee of Vice-Chancellors and Principals' retreat at Oxford (27–29 September, 1988) the Secretary of State for Education affirmed that the Government had accepted the key principles of the Higginson Report, and intended to use AS levels as the chief instrument in achieving a sixth-form curriculum which combined breadth with depth. Mr Baker urged the vice-chancellors to ensure that their admissions tutors asked university candidates for combinations of A and AS levels which would secure the balance of breadth and depth appropriate for the courses they seek to enter. Certainly, admissions tutors, in particular, need to be better informed about syllabus and curriculum developments. Lack of contact between university departments and the schools and examining boards leads to inflexible admissions policies, built on a combination of benign ignorance and prejudice.

However, at this particular historical moment the role of the universities should not be simply one of adjustment to the prevailing winds of change, from whichever direction. One of the ironies of the current situation in education generally, and in English studies in particular, is that the radical Left critique threatens to become dangerously complicit with that of the radical Right. The most alarming aspect of the Left's attack on the overdetermination of A-level English by the universities' 'élitist views of literary studies which privilege the literary text of the cultural heritage, above all other forms of discourse' (Goddard, p. 19), is that it coincides with a number of other interventions in the curriculum, many of them from the radical Right, which threaten to drive out the study of literature *however* defined.

First, there is the National Curriculum, which promises to improve literacy by giving English a key role as a core foundation subject. While most teachers of English will endorse the Government's commitment to improving standards of literacy, few will derive much comfort from the apparently newly enhanced status granted to their subject, for it is an extremely functionalist view of English and English teaching that is envisaged. For the present Government the chief function of English 11–16 seems to be to provide training in a narrow range of skills useful to employers. However, it is to be hoped that the judicious and wide ranging view of English offered in the recent report of the National Curriculum working party on English 5–11 will exert an influence on the shape of the curriculum 11–16.[8]

TVEI is also likely to have an adverse influence on the nature and function of English teaching. TVEI is a direct Government intervention in the curriculum which attempts to buy directly from schools what local education authorities have previously failed to deliver; it attempts to ensure that 80 per cent of school-leavers will enter the labour market with an employment-linked qualification acquired during full-time education. In short, it is a means of diverting a significant part of the work and resources of schools away from the educational needs and capacities of children towards the training needs of industry.

The allocations of curriculum time within the National Curriculum when combined with the demands on teaching time made by the technological and training components of TVEI will have the effect of severely curtailing the time available for humanities subjects. Many teachers fear that in this situation work in and with literature will have a greatly diminished role in the 11–16 curriculum. For most pupils

English could become a single-certificated subject at GCSE. English literature would thus become the exclusive preserve of a handful of fifth and sixth formers, and university students of English would become an even smaller, and presumably diminishing élite (or rump).

In addition to these threats to the space for English, and especially literature, in the curriculum there is also a potential threat to the English teacher's role in developing specialist syllabuses. It is clear from those sections of the National Curriculum consultation document dealing with assessment and examinations that the Government intends to take a great deal more central control of the examination boards than at present. For example, paragraph 33 on 16 + qualifications:

> At age 16, GCSE and other qualifications at equivalent level will provide the main means of assessment through examinations. But in order to ensure that the qualifications offered to pupils support or form part of the national curriculum attainment targets and programmes of study, the Government proposes to take powers to specify what qualifications may be offered to pupils during compulsory schooling. It also proposes to put onto a statutory footing the approval of syllabuses or courses leading to qualifications . . . (p. 16).

Post-16 qualifications will also be subject to greater uniformity and central control as they are brought under the regulation of the statutory SEAC (Schools Examination and Assessment Council) which will replace the non-statutory SEC (Secondary Examinations Council). Although the Higginson Committee's main recommendations on the need for a wider range of leaner, tougher A levels did not find favour with the Prime Minister, she is more likely to be moved by the housekeeperly rhetoric of economising and tidying up in its comments on the proposed review of A-level syllabuses.

> There are far too many A-level syllabuses . . . An enormous amount of effort goes in to drawing up and mounting something like 400 separate but often overlapping syllabuses. The education system can ill afford such extravagant use of resources, particularly human resources (Higginson, para. 5. 10).

It can be argued that many of the actual advances in A level have come from this 'extravagant' use of human resources in greater teacher involvement in the construction of syllabuses at all levels. Certainly it is uneconomic and educationally unproductive to have a system which fosters an apparently endless proliferation of syllabuses and Alternatives with their attendant problems of lack of coherence and conformity between boards. However, there are equal, perhaps greater dangers in the proposal that A-level syllabuses should be controlled by a statutory, government agency whose main aim is to produce an efficiently trained workforce to serve 'the economy'.

Not only is the content of A-level syllabuses under scrutiny, but also the constituency for A level. There are already a number of other qualifications such as BTEC (Business and Technician Education Council) and CPVE (Certificate of Pre-Vocational Education) on offer to full-time post-16 students in schools and colleges. In such courses English is replaced by Communications, the one thing needful to deliver the majority curriculum from an irrelevant minority culture, according to such advocates as Douglas Barnes and John Dixon. However the Communications approach, at least in its BTEC and CPVE guises, can all too easily be appropriated for the purposes of drilling students in the routines of linguistic exchange necessary for the efficient functioning of a hierarchic workplace, instead of developing an informed and critical awareness of their own and others' language uses.

In so far as these new courses have extended educational opportunities beyond the minority who currently pass A levels they must be welcomed. However, if these alternative 16 + and 18 + qualifications were to become the usual destination of a growing proportion of sixth formers in state schools and colleges, with A levels reserved for a diminishing and narrowly defined academic minority, then there would be real cause for concern. It is not immediately obvious that this is the best way of improving educational standards and opportunities for all, and it could well be a means of producing an increasingly stratified system of secondary education. Sir Maurice Shock has recently pointed out that the adoption of GCSE and the decision to retain traditional A levels might 'divide secondary education in new and damaging ways'.

If that does happen, the implications for the universities will be considerable. For example, there will be many schools which will assume that A levels are the main target of almost all their pupils from 14 onwards, with GCSE viewed more or less as only a stopping halt along the way. But it is already evident that a large number of schools will operate differently with GCSE as the primary aim to be followed for most of their pupils not by A levels but by one of the other post-16 qualifications now on offer (*TES*, 28.10.88).

In this situation universities might be tempted, unwisely in Shock's view, to regard the pupils taking the direct A-level route as their natural constituency. This would almost certainly have the effect of taking the universities back to the pre-Robbins era; there would be fewer, smaller universities. Few can imagine that this would be a better world. However, there is no doubt that for many departments, in many subjects, the recruitment of students who have followed the other route will have serious implications for the content and structure of their courses, as well as their teaching and assessment methods. Universities may no longer expect the curriculum for 16–19-year-olds to have as its main aim the preparation of students for higher education, but must be prepared to work with students from a wide range of educational backgrounds.[9] If this is to be the case, then universities would be unwise to maintain their customary distance from discussions about the shape and content of the 16–19 curriculum, especially its so-called non-academic branches.

For English studies these are troubled times. Starved of resources, besieged by a hostile, philistine ideology from Government, and even, on occasion, from within their own ranks, few English teachers can derive much sustenance from the claim made by recent secretaries of state to give a high priority to the teaching of English. There is, however, one benefit we may collectively derive from the current ferment; we may re-examine our assumptions and practices, re-assess our priorities, and redefine our projects. We must be prepared to ask 'for whose benefit Schools of English exist', and to acknowledge that to do so,

> is not to deny their importance as 'centres of excellence' in their own right, or to adopt a philistine approach which denies the intrinsic value of studying great literature . . . [But] if schools of literature are to exist, as they should, for the benefit of the whole community, they should concern themselves less narrowly with 'English Literature' and more with English in its multifarious and interdependent forms (Hollindale, p. 39).

In the face of increasingly functionalist definitions of English, university teachers of English should work with their colleagues in the schools to keep the multifarious and interdependent forms of English, including the literatures of English, both on the agenda and in the curriculum. The task is urgent if we are to continue to provide students in schools and universities not simply with the skills with which to function efficiently in a complex technological society, but rather with the knowledge and power with which to 'make sense of their worlds, to determine their own interests, both individual and collective, to see through the manipulations of all sorts of texts in all sorts of media, and to express their own views in [an] appropriate manner' (Scholes, pp. 15–16).

## Acknowledgement

I should like to thank Dr Bernard Harrison, Department of Educational Studies, University of Sheffield for his advice at an early stage in work for this essay.

## Abbreviations

| | |
|---|---|
| AEB | The Associated Examining Board |
| JMB | Joint Matriculation Board |
| SUJB | Southern Universities Joint Board |
| TES | *The Times Educational Supplement* |

## Notes

1 Common Statement of Aims of the GCE Boards of England, Wales, and Northern Ireland, reprinted in V. J. Lee, pp. 406–9.

2 These figures are taken from the statistical tables that form the appendix to the Higginson Report.

3 See M. A. K. Halliday *et al.*, *The Linguistic Sciences and Language Teaching* (Longman, 1964).

4 See Robert Protherough, 'Who Become Students of English?'

5 *TES*, 29.1.1988.

6 Readers of the National Curriculum Consultation Document will know that we now inhabit the world of market-education, whose relationships are defined in terms of 'providers', and 'clients' or 'consumers'. Strangely, the consumers of education are not, as one might expect, pupils, but rather parents and industrialists.

7 Peter Hollindale (see references below) suggests that the universities often work against cultural vitality. 'How much are universities, through the powerful downward pressures they exert, actually responsible for that impoverishment of general culture which they spend so much time lamenting?'

<sup>8</sup> See *English for Ages 5 to 11*, Report of the National Curriculum Working Party chaired by C. B. Cox (H.M.S.O., 1988).

<sup>9</sup> The growing importance of mature students will similarly require university departments to rethink their course structure and teaching methods.

## *References*

David Allen, *English Teaching Since 1965—How Much Growth?* (Heinemann, 1980).

Douglas R. Barnes *et al.*, *Versions of English* (Heinemann, 1984).

John Brown and Terry Gifford, 'Creative Responses in the Sixth Form', reprinted in V. J. Lee, 370–381.

G. Crowther, *15 to 18; a report of the Central Advisory Council for Education (England)* (H.M.S.O., 1959).

Peter Daw, 'There is an Alternative', *English in Education* 20:2 (1986), 63–71.

John Dixon *et al.*, *Education 16–19: the Role of English and Communication* (Macmillan, 1979).

Roy Goddard, 'Beyond the Literary Heritage: Meeting the needs in English Literature 16–19', *English in Education*, 19:2 (1985), 12–22.

G. Higginson, *Advancing A Levels: report of a committee appointed by the Secretary of State for Education and Science and the Secretary of State for Wales* (H.M.S.O., 1988).

Peter Hollindale, 'University English and the Sixth Form', *Use of English*, 37:2 (1986), 29–42.

V. J. Lee, *English Literature in Schools*, Exploring the Curriculum Series, (Open University Press, 1987).

Margaret Mathieson, *The Preachers of Culture: A Study of English and its Teachers* (Allen and Unwin, 1975).

*The National Curriculum 5–16: A Consultation Document* (H.M.S.O., 1987).

H. Newbolt, *The Teaching of English in England* (H.M.S.O., 1921).

J. Newsom, *Half Our Future: A report of the Central Advisory Council for Education (England)* (H.M.S.O., 1963).

Margaret Peacock and Elaine Scarratt, 'Changing Literature at "A" level', *Literature and History* 13:1 (1987), 104–115.

Robert Protherough, 'Who Become Students of English?', *English in Education* 21:2 (1987), 67–75.

W. A. Reid, *The Universities and the Sixth Form Curriculum*, Schools Council Research Studies (Macmillan, 1972).

Robert Scholes, *Textual Power, Literary Theory and the Teaching of English* (Yale University Press, 1985).

Andrew Spicer, 'Beyond the Critical Essay: "A" level English', *Use of English* 38:3 (1987), 20–28.

# What Happens to English Graduates?

## PETER CORBIN

Since 1981 British universities have had to face cuts in state funding and a consequent radical restructuring. The Government's 'philosophy' has been to encourage the universities, and higher education institutions generally, to organise and develop their affairs with a greater responsiveness to commercial and market forces than had previously been the case. Thus it has been suggested that universities and departments should endeavour to generate an increasing element of their financial support from, for example, research contracts with industry and commerce, from fund-raising and from the recruitment of overseas students who pay high tuition fees. In this way, it has been argued, universities should gain an increasing independence from state control and state interference in their affairs. This radical recasting of the British higher education system is far from over; currently a research selectivity exercise is being mounted to assess the research efficiency of universities and departments, the results of which will, in part, determine the level of Government support for individual institutions.

Of even greater significance, perhaps, are current ideas on the financial support of students, for in future it is likely that students, or their parents, will themselves have to bear an increasing proportion of the cost of their higher education via loans or their private income. One of the arguments in support of such a change is that students who are spending their *own* money will have a much sharper interest in choosing the subject which they wish to read and the department to which they apply. In this way individual disciplines and departments will need to take account of market forces, and among those market forces lie the applicant's expectations of his or her future career and its financial rewards on gaining a degree. A strong belief in market forces would suggest that the greatest employment rewards would be offered in areas of the greatest shortage and that young people, considering their future careers, should organise their university applications accordingly. Thus the employment market should exert a strong influence on the structuring of universities and the courses which English departments offer. In these circumstances it is important that individual disciplines have some sense of the employment destination of their

43

graduates, and especially so in the case of such disciplines as English which are not primarily vocational subjects and whose graduates frequently need to embark on further training, which in future may be costly, before entering employment.

It is extremely difficult to provide a comprehensive and accurate account of the 'destinations' of English students after graduation. Such information as is available is collected six months after the completion of their courses and at a time when a large number of graduates have yet to choose or settle into a career pattern. In their first year after graduation many students take up temporary employment, travel abroad or, having initially taken up an appointment, change their minds on career choice and move to another position. Subsequent or final 'destinations' often remain unrecorded and are thus something of a mystery unless or until reference requests are received, or unless individual members of academic staff maintain contact. Furthermore UGC statistics provide very limited information and inadequate breakdown of career 'destination', whilst information collected by careers offices is also limited by the response rate to enquiries and, in any case, is co-ordinated and analysed across the university sector in very selective detail. Thus this chapter can provide only a narrow and somewhat impressionistic sense of the overall pattern of English graduate employment and further training since much of the individual detail has had to be drawn from one university English department, which, however, is unlikely to be atypical. Finally the focus of analytical discussion has been confined to single-honours students since the information on combined-honours graduates is even more fragmented and difficult to extrapolate.

As we shall see, English graduates take up a wide variety of occupations and professions, and whilst only a minority may make direct formal use of their specifically literary skills and knowledge, the more *general* skills which they acquire in the course of their undergraduate career are held in high regard by employers. A recent article in *The Sunday Times*[1] suggested that narrow, directly relevant skills were regarded as a poor reason for taking someone on. Brian Corby, of The Prudential, was quoted as saying that his company had identified thirteen key 'competencies' which fall into six categories: communication, motivation, personal qualities, interpersonal skills, decision making, and management. Qualities included within these categories were the ability to listen, think about what is being said and reply to it effectively; attention to detail; responsiveness to new ideas; the ability to gather information systematically from a variety of sources in order to formulate a course of action; and the ability to establish priorities, schedule tasks and complete them on time. Colin Wheeler, of British Rail, was also quoted as stressing the importance of communications skills, creativity, original thinking and imagination. In addition the article suggested that good marks for dissertations and written work were highly rated by employers as evidence of an applicant's ability to observe deadlines and set his or her own standards. Many of these attributes are those which we would expect to find in a good humanities student and encouraged by a humanities undergraduate course and, most especially perhaps, in university English courses which are designed, among other things, to develop communications and interpersonal skills, imagination and creativity.

The current philosophy, that of the predominance of market forces and thus the demands and expectations of the recruitment market, has been continually stressed by the Government and its agencies. However, English departments and universities generally have also to respond to the market for student applications, not only in terms of numbers, but also in terms of the quality of the applicants. Admissions tutors would confirm that English is currently a popular subject which attracts applications from candidates with potential or achieved high scores at A level. In 1987 4791 candidates applied via UCCA for admission to English courses and the average AL score of the 2686 successful applicants was 11.6,[2] a score only exceeded by a small number of subjects such as medicine, veterinary science, mathematics and law.

Although related, the market forces operating on undergraduate applications over against the employment market have very different characteristics and impulses, and are to some extent opposed. Both admissions tutors and employers are concerned to attract highly motivated and intelligent applicants. However, most university applicants for English remain committed to the subject, the criteria which influence them to choose the discipline as a degree course are varied, and a consideration of their future career is only *one* factor among many. Most candidates at interview express a strong commitment to literary studies and a wish to extend their knowledge and experience of the subject, a liking for or proficiency in the discipline, together with a desire to obtain a good degree as a basis for further training and study. To judge from the section of the UCCA form which asks for career choice few candidates have made firm decisions, although many express an interest in employment areas such as the media and publishing, which are extremely difficult to enter. Few students, although they are an increasing minority, specifically ask about the employment record of and prospects for English graduates. Thus the majority of candidates and students appear to recognise that English is, for most of them, a non-vocational subject and that further study or training will be needed before they enter employment, and it is generally in the second year of their undergraduate career that students give serious thought to these issues.

The raw statistics[3] suggest that over the last several years an increasing proportion of English graduates immediately entered permanent UK employment. In 1982, 32% did so, whilst by 1986 the proportion had increased to 39.8%. Graduates taking up short-term UK employment increased from 3.9% to 6.1% over the same period, whilst those embarking upon teacher training dropped from 16.5% to 11.4%. Those entering upon further academic study showed a small increase, from 8.8% to 9.8%, whilst graduates receiving other training showed some decline from 13.1% in 1982 to 11.1% in 1986, with a peak in 1983 of 14.4%. A small number of graduates, 3.5% to 4.5%, found employment abroad over the period, whilst the proportion unemployed after six months fell from 18% in 1982 to 10.8% in 1986.

The most popular first destinations for English students immediately entering employment on graduation (39.8% in 1986), are sales and marketing (17.7%), administration and management (16.8%), financial work (13.5%) and literary, entertainment and other creative work (13.5%). A further sector which has attracted English graduates has been health and social welfare, although this has suffered a sharp decline.

Such statistics give a very limited view of the variety of individual occupations available to English students, but they do suggest that those skills which students acquire in their undergraduate career—the ability to appraise material and information, to present their views articulately both on paper and in discussion, to organise and prioritise their activities without close supervision and so on—are marketable.

The first destination of English graduates from Exeter broadly conforms to the national pattern, although the 1987 survey showed a larger proportion in short-term employment, lower numbers in sales and marketing and teacher training, although a similar proportion found positions in the very competitive literary and entertainment areas. Two graduates found their way into the acting profession, two into journalism, one of them a sports reporter, and another joined Virago Press as an editorial assistant. Finance also proved a popular destination with a number of graduates becoming accountancy trainees, account executives and one joining the Stock Exchange as a broker/market maker. The Civil Service also attracted graduates, one working in the Crown Prosecution Service; others took up managerial and public relations training or posts. Two graduates found a place in the legal world, one working for Bar Finals and the other taking articles with a firm of solicitors.

Of those taking further full-time study five embarked on higher degrees, one an MSc in Information Technology; only three joined courses for the Post-Graduate Certificate of Education, the qualification for teaching in schools, with one student in temporary work before taking a teaching course; one studied for a TEFL (Teaching of English as a Foreign Language) diploma and another followed a course in the History of Fine and Decorative Arts. Only two graduates took secretarial training, a marked decrease on the earlier 1980s. It should also be remembered that the majority of English graduates are women (66.7% in 1986) and that their working careers are likely to be interrupted or curtailed by family responsibilities. Their contribution to the 'economic' health of our society must not be underestimated. Rearing children is an immeasurable contribution to society and many will return to employment and bring with them much-needed skills.

The 1988 survey, although incomplete, suggests a similar variety of destinations. Six graduates are pursuing post-graduate degrees, one is on a diploma course in publishing, another has entered drama school, and only *one* has taken up teacher training. The financial industry has again attracted applicants; three graduates have joined firms of accountants and two the insurance industry. Two have taken up management posts, one has found a post in market research and another in sales. Two graduates are working in journalism, three in publishing, and two others have jobs as DJs with local radio stations. Other posts include computer programming, legal work, and teaching English abroad.

It must be stressed again that two surveys taken six months after graduation provide a limited view of the employment pattern of English graduates. However, previous surveys confirm a similar range of posts, in librarianship, advertising, computers, local radio, television, the insurance industry, museum work, the Health Service, the armed forces, the police, etc. None the less such surveys are a fallible guide to subsequent graduate employment. The student who, six months after graduation, was in temporary work eventually turns out to be the producer of the BBC's most popular radio soap opera, the student who joined the accountancy firm with such enthusiasm later writes for a reference for a PGCE course, and the student who initially entered teacher training now writes music criticism for *The Times* and *The Gramophone*. The employment market is very mobile and English graduates, as with graduates in general, are likely to be in increasingly short supply. One of my students, a graduate of two years, recently took a post with an advertising agency at a salary in excess of £16,000, and, with such financial rewards available, movement in employment is likely to increase. Potential employers are now well aware of this and are beginning to organise their recruitment of graduates with elaborate and expensive public relations exercise. Some firms are targeting their recruitment on specific universities. Others are offering undergraduate prizes, linked to employment advice and academic support, in order to make early contact with those students who are likely to be academically successful. The economy's appetite for graduate skills is likely to continue to expand and ensure a wide range of employment opportunities for graduates in English, since English attracts applicants of high potential and offers undergraduate courses which encourage and teach highly marketable skills.

*Notes*

[1] Godfrey Golzen, 'So just what is a "relevant" study?', 11 December 1988.

[2] *UCCA Statistical Supplement, 25th Report 86–87*, UCCA. The highest possible score of three A levels would be 15.

[3] Information drawn from *What Do Graduates Do?* published by the Association of Careers Advisory Services.

# Language and Literature in English Studies
## RONALD CARTER

## 1.0 *Introduction*

This chapter has the following main aims: to discuss, with particular reference to the field of *stylistics*, the developments in English studies which have led to a fuller integration of language and literary studies; to outline the growth of modern English language studies in departments of English Language and Literature in senior school and higher education sectors, with particular reference to recently published government reports into the teaching of English language; and to evaluate the implications for curriculum development in English studies of advances in these domains.

Such a project is a relatively ambitious one for the available space and is necessarily prone to generalisation; suggestions for further reading are, however, liberally interspersed throughout the paper.

## 1.1 *Stylistics*

The subject of stylistics is not a new one. Its roots lie in research into style by literary linguists in the Moscow and Prague Philological Circles during the twenties and thirties—work which was developed by major figures in the field such as Leo Spitzer in the forties and fifties.[1] The institutionalisation of the subject in academic courses proceeded during the sixties and seventies with the result that many departments of English Studies or Humanities in universities and polytechnics now have courses entitled 'literary linguistics' 'literary language' or 'stylistics' which apply techniques derived from linguistic analysis to what is argued to be a more than usually detailed and systematic interpretation of the part played by language in the creation of textual meanings. The marriage of linguistics and literary studies has not been without its disputes, both ideological and territorial, (for a representative discussion see chapters in Roger Fowler's *Language of Literature*);[2] and there have been partings of the ways. There have been numerous signs, however, of increasing reconciliations and new alignments.

Much of the impetus to fuller integration can be traced to two main developments in literary linguistic studies during the late seventies and during the eighties: an openness to new directions in literary theory and a broadening of the parameters of analysis and discussion to include notions of *discourse*. Of these the growth in the study of discourse has been the most significant. One of the main reasons why the analysis of discourse has served in a unifying role is that the domains of language and discourse are central to the study of texts and the organisation of texts.

For literary and linguistic scholars, however, the term discourse has different inflections which it may be helpful to attempt to clarify. Within linguistics discourse analysis is a useful umbrella term which covers the study of language beyond the level of the sentence. This means that the focus is on: the larger macrostructural patterns of *written* language which obtain in such units as paragraphs, textual categories such as openings or abstracts, and genres such as instruction, report or narrative; as well as on those patterns of *spoken* language organisation which obtain beyond the boundaries of single conversational turns in realms which are variously termed exchanges, stretches of talk or conversational sequences. This focus does not exclude grammar or phonology, for both will be significant in the communication of discoursal meanings, but such patterns are essentially microstructural patterns. Microstructural patterns are important for the expression of delicate meanings, and stylistics based on grammar and phonology has contributed much to our understanding of such literary effects as metrical and sound patterns in poetry, tense in the novel and so on. But stylistics has been frequently charged with being too narrowly based. Discourse stylistics, which draws on developments in discourse analysis, lays a systematic basis for exploring the larger functions of language and thus such effects and formal categories as point of view and speech presentation, dialogue, dramatic interaction, narrative organisation—areas of semiosis which are central and will continue to be central to the concerns of students and researchers of literature.[3] The study of literary texts as sites for the analysis of patterns of discourse is in many areas still in its formative stages but throughout the eighties it has revealed itself as a source of mutual interest and enrichment on both sides of what is increasingly less of a linguistic literary divide.

An openness to new developments in literary theory has also promoted rather more extensive integration of linguistic and literary studies. Some pedagogical implications of such openness and influence will be discussed below but some of the most significant results in terms of theory and analytical practice can be outlined briefly here. These include an examination of the nature of literariness in language. The questioning within literary theory of the nature of literature itself, the construction and deconstruction of literary canons and the study of the varying reception of literature relative to social context has led stylisticians to embrace a much wider range of texts as sources of 'literariness'. It is now not uncommon for jokes, popular fiction and advertising language to be analysed alongside a Shakespearean sonnet or an opening to a novel by Jane Austen, leading to the replacement of literature by the term 'text' and aligning some stylisticians with developments within 'English' which are now more properly termed cultural studies. Other influences from within literary theory have led to greater recognition of the provisionality of interpretation and thus to less grandiose claims to the accessing of 'meaning' through wholly text-intrinsic linguistic means.

A further significant influence is that of work on *discourse* and literary theory. Work within this tradition is different from discourse analysis within linguistics but there is considerable potential for convergence of interests. The exploration of discourse in this connection is that associated with the French literary and social theorist Michel Foucault.

Foucault's primary work was undertaken in the seventies but his influence has come to be exerted on literary stylistics during the eighties. Foucault's view of 'discourse' is that of a set of historically variable determinations. For him there is no single right way to see things, no single position from which 'reality' can be interpreted. Our knowledge and beliefs, Foucault argues, are discursively produced, that is, they are not universal but are historically and culturally shaped. This means that the meanings of texts can only be interpreted relative to the discourses available and thus that language does not mediate reality in any simple common-sense or 'transparent' way. Instead it is a site in and through which ideologies are refracted. Under Foucault's influence there is an increasing move towards stylistic analysis of literary texts which are predominantly concerned with socio-semiotic and socio-historical meaning relations.[4]

A related influence from within linguistics rather than from within literary and cultural theory has been the critical linguistics associated with Roger Fowler. Fowler demonstrates that stylistic analysis can and should be applied more generally than to the works conventionally designated 'literary' and argues that division between literary and non-literary texts is an arbitrary one and that the literary should not be privileged. Fowler accepts Foucault's position that meanings are not text-intrinsic and that textual critics should concentrate on using linguistic techniques as a means of uncovering and interpreting the value systems and ideologies which inform the text.[5]

If ways can be found of systematically relating configurations of discourse to particular linguistic realisations in macrostructural patterns of language in literary and non-literary texts then the marriage of linguistics and literary studies may become such that even notions of partnership and mutuality might be displaced by a much fuller unification. It must be recognised, however, that projects of this kind are limited and preliminary at this time.[6]

## 2.0  *Modern English Language Studies*

One of the aims of stylistics is to effect an integration of language and literary studies. In so doing developments in stylistics will feed from and feed into studies in Modern English Language. Modern English Language Studies remains, however, a separate and distinctive area with lines of demarcation drawn in both theory and practice with the cognate domains of literary studies, linguistics and the more established domain of historical and philological language study.

Among the most significant of developments in Modern English Language Studies during the eighties have been: an increase in studies in *language variation*, both in terms of accent/dialect variation and variation in written text types; explorations in the relationship between *language and ideology*; investigations of the relationship between language and social context. Here it will be seen that the main developments have been broadly sociolinguistic and discoursal and in this regard the tendency has been to follow and incorporate developments in systemic-functional linguistics directed largely under the influence of Michael Halliday[7] rather than the more psycholinguistically-inspired, universalising cognitive linguistics directed largely under the influence of the American linguist Noam Chomsky.

Alongside such theoretical and descriptive interests there have also grown up in recent Modern English Language Studies distinctive methodological orientations. These affect, in particular, the kinds of data collected and the ways in which such data are scrutinised. The most important consideration is the collection of naturally occurring data. That is, the language data or textual examples to be analysed are obtained in *real* contexts of use. They are not made up by linguists in the comfort of their own studies and with access only to their own intuitions as to the authenticity of the data. Students and researchers in Modern English Language are more interested in the genuine relationships which inhere between language and its users and the social contexts in which it is embedded, entailing as it does much fuller reference to the counterbalancing and intersubjective role of informants' judgements and intuitions. Such non-idealised data is necessarily complicated but it is at least authentic and descriptions of it are therefore argued to be of much more use to the study of the social functions of language or of the effects of such language in contexts of discourse. A further fundamental methodological principle is that language research should be 'scientific' in so far as intuitions are followed, hypotheses constructed, data collected and data examined in the light of the hypotheses, especially with reference to informants' judgements. These processes result not only in the formulation of discourse-sensitive theory but in the continuous adaptation and refinement of relevant descriptive frameworks. Such an overall emphasis on the enabling functions of descriptive frameworks also lends itself to an investigative, empirical, project-based approach to language study—an approach which has important repercussions for pedagogies of Modern English Language Studies (see 3.1).

The area of Modern English Language Studies has recently received considerable support in the form of a government Committee of Inquiry set up under the chairmanship of Sir John Kingman[8] and with the following terms of reference:

1. To recommend a model of the English language, whether spoken or written, which would:
   (i) serve as the basis of how teachers are trained to understand how the English language works;
   (ii) inform professional discussion of all aspects of English teaching.

2. To recommend the principles which should guide teachers on how far and in what ways the model should be made explicit to pupils, to make them conscious of how language is used in a range of contexts.

3. To recommend what, in general terms, pupils need to know about how the English language works and in consequence what they should have been taught, and be expected to understand, on this score, at age 7, 11, and 16.

The Kingman Report is of immediate relevance to English language teaching in schools and the Cox committee established three months after the publication of the report of the Kingman committee was charged with developing some of the main recommendations of Kingman into a more systematic, linguistically informed basis for a national curriculum for English and for the training of teachers of English. As far as higher education is concerned the Kingman committee's recommendations are not without relevance for English Language Studies within departments where English is studied in whole or in part for a first degree. In chapter 6 paragraph 11 the following recommendation is made:

> The Committee recommends that before the end of the century a prerequisite for entry to the teaching profession as an English specialist should normally be a first degree in English which incorporates a study of contemporary and historical linguistic form and use.[9]

It should be pointed out here that, notwithstanding such integrative work as outlined above, some departments of 'English' do exist where the exclusive preoccupation is with literature or with cultural studies and in which the study of language is at best peripheral to other concerns.

Within the profession of Modern English Language teachers the Report of the Kingman Inquiry has received a broad welcome. The suggested model of the English language is agreed to offer a sound basis for both descriptive and pedagogic development and the advocacy of a view of language as discourse (with appropriate descriptive frameworks) and of stylistic analysis as an integrative component in language and literary studies courses and as a corrective to more impressionistic language-based criticism is in tune with contemporary teaching and research developments.

The report is, however, neglectful of the role of literary theory at the interface of language and literary studies and adopts a markedly centrist monolingual and monocultural view of English as language and literature. The following omissions and elisions from the report should be also particularly noted:

1. *Literature as decontextualised* A 'decontextualised' view of literature is one in which what counts are the words on the page rather than the social and political conditions under which the texts and their words are produced. The dangers here are those associated with New Criticism and Traditional Stylistics: texts are seen to exist in a kind of vacuum, a social and cultural space disinfected of historical determinants. Kingman takes a generally decontextualised view of literary artefacts.

2. *Meanings are 'eternal'* One result of the above decontextualisation is that texts are read as having unchanging 'eternal' meanings (see particularly p. 27 para 18 of the report and the discussion of 'eternal truths' and 'eternal worlds'). Students need to be shown that meanings are produced not given.

3. *Readers as asocial* There is some recognition in the report that writers write within an 'external' context (p. 27) by which is meant, we presume, a social and historical context. But readers are constructed as primarily empirical psychological respondents reading in order to locate the 'internal context' of the text, in order to realise its power to 'stir, entertain and move' (see p. 42 para 27). Reading involves psychological processes such as allowing images to expand and resonate in the mind (p. 28, making imaginative efforts to respond to *the* message (sic) and reaching the '*correct* understanding' (*sic*). There is little recognition in the report that reading as a woman or as an immigrant or as a conservative voter may result in different interpretations because of different *social* experiences and positions. Much recent literary theoretical work demonstrates the impossibility of reading asocially or ahistorically and underlines how interpretation involves social as well as psychological processes. Reading texts with close attention to language must be primary but it would be dangerous if texts were taught as if they had single 'eternal' meanings. Interpretation is ineluctably conditioned by a *variety* of factors such as race, social class, gender, religious beliefs and so on.

4. *Form and meaning are unilinear* This is a further assumption underlying New Critical and Traditional Stylistic practice: that certain forms produce certain meanings. Thus, a particular linguistic feature of a text such as the deletion from that text of a main finite verb (cf. the opening to *Bleak House*) is assumed to have a particular single meaning or effect. In the committee's commentary on the opening to *Bleak House* the effect is identified as one of 'static eternity'; but it could just as easily be interpreted as producing a sense of disorientation and disorder, of narratorial impersonality or the effect of a disinterested inventory. Much will depend on the constellation of other linguistic effects in the passage. Such a practice (of assuming unilinear correlations of form and meaning), which is quite widespread in the Kingman commentaries, leads with little resistance to a further bracketing out of an already decontextualised reader, to a potentially dangerous recognition that there is a 'right' interpretation and to teacher-centred methodologies (where the teacher is in sole possession

of the answer). Recent publications by Stanley Fish among others have demonstrated the naivety of such reading practices and shown how they can be deconstructed.[10]

To repeat, however, the report of the Kingman Inquiry into English Language teaching, although not altogether alert to recent developments in the study of language in relation to literature, has done much to reinsert questions of English language, especially modern English language use, into the development of the English curriculum at all levels.

## 3.0 *Curriculum development*

Much can be learned about the curriculum for English Language Studies from consideration of the kinds of questions which students are invited to answer. The examples examined below are taken from GCE Advanced Level examinations in English Language. The questions provide some indication of the required competences of students at pre-university levels but also an example of the kinds of orientation to language study influenced by developments in higher education, although the relationship is reversed in the case of some universities and colleges with A level providing a basis for university curriculum renewal and reform. We shall also explore briefly in this section two other main areas of curriculum design in language and literary studies in higher education: the rediscovery of rhetoric in relation of stylistics in courses in composition and writing and the influence of developments in teaching literature to students for whom English is not a first language.

## 3.1 *Examining English language*

The following sample examination questions are taken from the 1946 University of London General Secondary Education English Language paper (I) and the 1984 University of London GCE A-level Varieties of English paper (II):

I (a) Analyse into clauses the following passage. Give the grammatical description of the clauses and show their connection with each other:

> In that year [1851] when the Great Exhibition spread its hospitable glass roof high over the elms of Hyde Park, and all the world came to *admire* England's wealth, progress and enlightenment, there might

*profitably* have been another 'exhibition' to show how our poor were housed and to teach the admiring foreign visitor *some* of the dangers *that* beset the path of the vaunted new era.

(b) State the grammatical features of the words italicised in (a)

II   In February 1984 all the national daily newspapers reported an incident which occurred at a colliery in Northumberland. The participants involved were the chairman of the National Coal Board (Mr Ian MacGregor), miners, and policemen.

The following reports from four of the daily papers deal with the same events, but are contrasted in their interpretation of what took place, and offer their readers different impressions.

(i) Examine and discuss the language of the reports in terms of their choices of vocabulary and grammar, and in the ordering of the events described. Relate these choices to the differences of interpretation presented by the papers, with reference to both the headlines and the reports.

(ii) Discuss some of the problems which may arise in 'reporting the facts' of a news item accurately and impartially. Say which of the reports seems to you to be prejudiced either for or against any of the participants, referring in detail to the linguistic evidence for your judgements.

Discuss at least three reports in some detail.

The two papers represent the shift in the field of Modern English Language Studies adumbrated at 2.0. above. The former exercise involves a naming and classification of grammatical forms in and for itself; the latter exercise also requires formal identification but focuses more explicitly on the functions realised by those forms and on the relationship between language (here particularly grammar) and the mediation of ideology. The former exercise is decontextualised; the latter is sensitive to the contexts in which language is used. Students are invited to see through language to the larger purposes to which it is put.

## 3.2   *Stylistics, composition and rhetoric*

Another marked trend in stylistics and language studies during the eighties has been a renewed interest in compositional processes. Stylisticians have repeatedly argued that to understand the workings of language and associated theories of language in written communication it is necessary to conduct analyses of different kinds of text. Stylisticians are now repeatedly arguing that to be properly acquainted with the lessons of analysis it is necessary to practice the actual making of texts. Thus composition is inextricably related with theory and description; theoretical and analytical concerns guide us towards facility in composition; composition is, in return, a kind of analysis.[11]

This theoretical position within language pedagogy finds expression in an increasing number of courses devoted to a fostering of compositional skills and to examinations in which writing is required of students in place of or prior to procedures of commentary and analysis. Space is limited for illustration but once more examples from examination papers give a synoptic view of course objectives and teaching methods. Here are two examples: from a JMB (Joint Matriculation Board) A-level English Language paper (A) and an undergraduate English examination in 'Stylistics and Composition' (B).

A. The BBC is planning a series of short programmes (15 to 20 minutes each) on momentous technological and scientific discoveries of the twentieth century. The series will emphasise the social consequences of invention and innovation and in particular will be concerned with their effects on human awareness and attitudes. The programmes will be broadcast on Radio Four under the general title of DECISIVE MOMENTS IN TWENTIETH CENTURY HISTORY.

Your task is to write the script for a programme on the first atomic bombs. You may choose whichever form and style you wish so long as the issues and events are clearly presented to the listener. Accurate attention to details is expected together with some provision of historical context. The producer has indicated however that he does not want a merely historical account of the dropping of the first bombs.

You are free to choose your own starting point and do not need to refer to any other programmes. You should include such incidents as you think will be effective but there is no obligation to cover all the events and personalities in the source material. Remember to give clear instructions for the presenters and for any other participants in the programmes, and to indicate sound effects where appropriate.

It should be noted here that examinees are provided with assignment source material, in the form of an extensive bank of relevant texts, 48 hours in advance of the examination in order to allow them to be thoroughly acquainted with and to have undertaken linguistic analysis of the data. It should also be noted that a second paper in the examination tests students' competence in more traditional forms of text-based analysis of language use, with particular reference to social and historical variation.

The second example (B) is more directly compositional *and* analytical involving the pedagogic strategies of paraphrase and rewriting.

B.  1. Here are lists of nouns, verbs and adverbs, presented in random order. Determine in each case a sequence indicative of a story or a narrative episode, and write a paragraph composing the narrative:

    (a) gale   hat   smile   cry   meeting
    (b) stretch   rise   stumble   curse   rinse
    (c) suspiciously   carefully   cautiously   timidly
    thankfully

    Now write either a brief cautionary tale or a newspaper report derived from the following set of sentences (which you may order as you please):

The policeman is watchful
The child is curious
The traffic is heavy
The gate is open
The mother is busy

The object of this exercise is twofold. One aim is to discover stimuli that may nudge you into composition. The other is to prompt a critical review of your compositional procedures. Try to understand the relationship between a proposed function (e.g. 'cautionary tale', 'newspaper report') and the language you select to express that function. Does your writing imply an appeal to a reader? If so, how is that appeal exercised? Do you find yourself using certain sentence-types, for example question-forms? What is the average length of your sentences? Do you tend to keep a mean length, or are there stylistically significant variations, e.g. through the abrupt introduction of a shorter-than-average?' Are the sentences notably complex in structure or do you confine yourself to fairly simple constructions? What have you done to make the text 'read' cohesively? How have you guided a potential reader through the text—what are its principles of design? Are there indications in your text of an orientation to time and place? Or to events, phenomena, and personalities 'outside' the text? What of the vocabulary? Are form-classes like the adjective and adverb prominent in your writing or do you prefer to make nouns and verbs do most of the communicative work? Is the vocabulary 'bookish' or 'colloquial', or a mixture of these? Is the appeal of the vocabulary sensory and emotive, or abstract and intellectual? Do you make much use of figurative language? Are your figures of speech conventional, or do they reflect your own figurative invention?

2.  Blank filling. Here is an outline for a piece of verse, in which line-beginnings and line-endings have been supplied. The line-beginnings are represented by various grammatical operators or structure words (articles, auxiliaries, pronouns, conjunctions); the line-endings present a rhyme pattern turning on words some of which are semantically related (as colour words) while the remainder are random selections. Complete the verse by filling in the intervening blanks in each line. You are free to choose your own line-length, metre, and prosodic stanza-pattern.

| | |
|---|---|
| There was | green |
| Whose | brown |
| His | queen |
| And | town |
| But though | red |
| Was | yellow |
| The | said |
| That | fellow |

N. B. Poetic quality is not required, though the verse should be metrical and make sense. The exercise demonstrates two kinds of constraint: the semantic limitations imposed by rhyme, and the syntactic constraints determined by the grammatical elements at the beginning of each line. If the task as it stands proves too difficult, try first cancelling the rhymes in favour of others of your own choice, while keeping the grammatical cues, then keeping the suggested rhymes but framing the verse in accordance with your own grammatical scheme.

3.  Rewrite the following passage, attempting to convey its sense while changing as far as possible the length, and construction of its sentences and paragraphs, and the ordering and prominence of the information it conveys. Change in syntax may occasionally necessitate changes in vocabulary, to raise the overall formality of the style:

**LOS ANGELES**—An 11-year-old girl noticed a 3-foot-tall marijuana plant growing in the back yard here this week and turned in her parents. Police are holding the girl in protective custody lest her parents speak sharply to her while an investigation continues.

This is evidence of drug abuse hysteria, as if the nation is on a high from its crackdown on crack.

No wonder. News magazines have been conducting a circulation-building war on drugs for months; television networks are finding prime-time slots for documentaries deploring the crisis; newspapers vie for the most lurid series on the local angle of the issue now in vogue.

Politicians know they can get on the air and in print by railing at the pushers at home and the producers abroad. Pollsters tell candidates that interest in drug abuse is number one on the voters' hit parade, and every commercial turns otherwise serious legislators into apoplectic cops demanding death penalties and bombing runs. With the media-political symbiosis running rampant at campaign time, news junkies ask: Is drug abuse worse now than a year ago? (Syndicated article by William Safire, *Seattle Post-Intelligencer*, 13 September 1986)

Your revised piece might begin thus:

In order to forestall retaliatory action during the course of their enquiries, Los Angeles police have taken into protective custody an 11-year-old girl who this week reported her parents after noticing a 3-foot-tall marijuana plant growing in the back yard. If this instance appears merely to support a general impression that the intensive campaign against 'crack' has produced a national state of hysteria over the abuse of drugs, there can be no wonder.

On the other hand, the aim of the rewriting might be to make the piece even more familiar and colloquial in tone. It might then begin thus:

That plant in your back yard. Three feet tall and flourishing. Have you ever thought what it might be? Better yet, have your *kids* ever thought what it might be? Just suppose it's marijuana, and let's pretend the little dears decide to turn mummy and daddy over to the law. Not so funny, eh? But that's exactly what happened in Los Angeles this week. An 11-year-old girl reported her parents for drug abuse. Now she is in custody. Protective custody. While mum and dad are under investigation. Just in case they get mad with her. And want to get even.

There's only one word for this sort of thing. HYSTERIA. And who is to blame?. . . .

4. Taking Wordsworth's sonnet 'Westminster Bridge':

> Earth has not anything to show more fair:
> Dull would he be of soul who could pass by
> A sight so touching in its majesty:
> This City now doth, like a garment, wear
> The beauty of the morning; silent, bare
> Ships, towers, domes, theatres and temples lie
> Open to the fields, and to the sky;
> All bright and glittering in the smokeless air.
> Never did sun more beautifully steep
> In his first splendour, valley, rock, or hill;
> Ne'er saw I, never felt, a calm so deep!
> The river glideth at his own sweet will:
> Dear God! the very houses seem asleep;
> And all that mighty heart is lying still.

(a) Attempt a prose paraphrase; then study the compromises and necessary defects of paraphrase.

(b) Make a prose version, faithful to the content of the poem but composed as though for an encyclopaedia entry ('the city is most advantageously viewed from one of the bridges, preferably in the early morning before traffic builds up'), or for a travel book ('we were struck by the almost rural calm of our surroundings'), or for a commercial ('you'll THRILL to the stupendous views!')

It will be seen from these examples that such linguistic activity parallels more traditional courses in rhetoric, especially those found in colleges and universities in the United States. It should be noted, too, that re-writing, paraphrase and related procedures can be applied to texts which carry particular social and political resonances; the resulting analysis and production of texts becomes one more fully based in the notion of rhetoric as social action.

## 3.2   *Language, literature and English as a foreign language: pedagogical stylistics*

The last ten years have seen an extensive application of studies and practices in stylistics to the teaching of English as a second or foreign language. This emergence of a new field of pedagogical stylistics is a part of the growth of the teaching of English to speakers of other languages, a growth which has been fed by a variety of determinants ranging from the rise of English as a world language and the consequent demand for courses designed for teachers in such contexts to the economic necessity for many British universities to recruit more higher-fee-paying students from overseas.

Much work in pedagogical stylistics has resulted in the re-insertion of literature into a second and foreign-language curriculum which has been dominated by narrower communicative and functional goals alongside which the teaching of literature was seen as either irrelevant or, at best, a luxury. Literary texts, it is argued in such contexts, can be deployed for purposes of developing interpretive skills through language in a more concentrated and intense way than is possible with non-literary material.[12] The last five years have seen an extension to the range of integrated language and literary materials for purposes of language learning and development, some of which are not without relevance for language pedagogies for students for whom English is a first language.[13]

Additionally, we should note the increases in integrated language and stylistic research into second-language literatures, that is, non-canonical literature in English produced in different world Englishes by writers selecting English as a medium for creative expression even though English is not their mother tongue.[14]

## 3.3   *Conclusion*

The last decade has seen a maturation of the relationship between language and literature. The advances in Modern English Language Studies which have resulted in an increasing attention in both research and teaching to language as a socially signifying practice have taken the subject beyond the dangers of excessive formalism towards a recognition that meanings are both provisional and relative to discourse contexts. This direction has also led literary critics increasingly to recognise the relevance of systematic accounts of linguistic patterning to their own concerns with textuality and the production of literary meanings. There is much still to be learned on both sides and much work still to be done before more are convinced of the mutual benefits but the more modern English language study develops as an independent academic domain the greater the possibilities for yet further integration.

## Notes

1 For a lucid and representative survey see David Birch, *Language, Literature and Critical Practice: Ways of Analyzing Text* (London, 1988).

2 Roger Fowler, *The Languages of Literature* (London, 1971). The book contains chapters which reprint a debate between the author and F. W. Bateson originally conducted in *Essays in Criticism*.

3 See Michael Toolan, *Narrative: A Critical Linguistic Introduction* (London, 1988); Ronald Carter and Paul Simpson (eds.) *Language, Discourse and Literature: An Introductory Reader in Discourse Stylistics* (London, 1989); Deirdre Burton, *Dialogue and Discourse* (London, 1980).

4 For a lucid introduction to Foucault's thinking see Alan Sheridan *Michel Foucault: The Will to Truth* (London, 1980) and Diane Macdonell, *Theories of Discourse* (Oxford, 1986).

5 See Roger Fowler, *Literature as Social Discourse* (London, 1981), *Linguistic Criticism* (Oxford, 1986).

6 Some exciting beginnings are, however, demonstrated in David Birch and Michael O'Toole (eds.) *The Functions of Style* (London, 1987). See, in particular, the essay 'Stories of Race and Gender' in this volume by Terry Threadgold.

7 Michael Halliday, *Language as Social Semiotic* (London, 1978); *An Introduction to Functional Grammar* (London, 1985).

8 *Report of the Committee of Inquiry into the Teaching of English Language* (under the chairmanship of Sir John Kingman) (London, HMSO, 1988).

9 Ibid p. 70.

10 Stanley Fish's criticisms of stylistics are contained in *Is There A Text in This Class?: The Authority of Interpretive Communities* (Cambridge, Mass. 1980).

11 A seminal and influential volume in 'compositional stylistics' is Walter Nash, *Designs in Prose* (London, 1980).

12 For representative arguments and pedagogic illustrations see H. G. Widdowson, *Stylistics and the Teaching of Literature* (London, 1975); Ronald Carter and Christopher Brumfit (eds.), *Literature and Language Teaching* (Oxford, 1986).

13 See John McRae and Roy Boardman, *Reading Between The Lines: Integrated Language and Literary Activities* (Cambridge, 1984); Ronald Carter and Michael Long, *The Web of Words: Exploring Literature Through Language* (Cambridge, 1987).

14 For example, essays in Larry Smith (ed.) *Discourse Across Cultures* (Oxford, 1987).

# English and Interdisciplinary Studies

## MICHAEL IRWIN

This chapter does not set out to advocate a particular view, nor to offer a full summary of pros and cons. Rather it presents a number of alternative lines of argument. Given the complexity of the issue it need not matter that these lines point in a confusing variety of directions. What is worrying is that several of them seem to point downwards. . . .

I

Universities change and disciplines change within them. The transforming impulses may be internal—academic or pedagogical—or external, in the shape of political or financial pressures or changing patterns of student demand. In Britain over the past thirty years influences particularly of the latter kind have transformed our tradition of higher education. Until the 1960s a small number of universities (twenty-odd) accommodated a bare four per cent of the relevant age-group. These select students, having enjoyed a specialised training in the relevant subject area from the age of sixteen, were well equipped to undertake an intensive, monodisciplinary three-year course. They could be supervised rather than taught. One doesn't have to endorse this tradition to recognise its coherence: it made sense on its own terms.

Over the past thirty years, however, these terms have been altered, piecemeal, beyond recognition. Universities have grown in size and doubled in number. The undergraduate intake has vastly increased and diversified, extending to part-time, mature and overseas students—some of them one-year visitors. For English departments, among others, the educational enterprise has therefore had to be redefined. Syllabus changes have meant that few first-year undergraduates have any knowledge of Latin or of classical mythology. Some will have studied no history to speak of; others will lack even a smattering of a foreign language. In many cases the only pre-nineteenth-century texts studied at school will have been a couple of Shakespeare's plays. The degree course still lasts three years, but it must take in far more preparatory work—including instruction in essay-writing and even syntax.

Meanwhile the subject has correspondingly grown and diversified. 'English Literature', in itself far too large a subject to be studied in three years, is tending to become 'Literatures in English', as it comprehends American, African, Caribbean or Australian writing. Literary Theory threatens something between amplification, restructuring and a complete takeover of the syllabus. Altogether it has become harder to reach even working departmental agreements about the nature of the discipline or the structure of the degree programme.

However, the great majority of English lecturers would instinctively concur about the building blocks from which such a programme would be principally constructed. The basic unit, which still feels sound, is a seminar on *Macbeth* or 'Michael' or *Middlemarch*. We know this educational experience makes sense because we've participated in it not only as teachers but as students—indeed it probably drew us into the profession in the first place. Most would agree that a related sequence of such seminars—courses in, say, Shakespeare, Romantic Poetry or Victorian Poetry, will similarly make sense, its constituent parts being cross-related and mutually reinforcing. The conceptual problem typically arises at the level of syllabus: that of mounting and grouping a *series* of such courses and defining the intellectual context that gives them collective significance.

In one sense, therefore, it's hardly an embarrassment to be faced with large numbers of applicants wishing to take a selection of such individual courses in combination with another subject rather than read English Literature alone. And the numbers *are* large: at the University of Kent, for example, one English application in three is for a joint-honours programme. For several reasons, that proportion is likely to increase rather than otherwise. Broader sixth-form syllabuses—perhaps the further spread of AS levels—will give students a range of subject interests that many will be reluctant to limit too far at university level. A feeling among arts students that they should, for economic reasons, be getting an education with a vocational flavour will lead a number of them to take, say, computing or accounting, but leaven it with Keats and Dickens. There is a related pressure within the university. Certain humanities subjects which have been running short of applicants badly need the 'half-students' they can attract to a joint-honours programme with English. For several external reasons, then, we are being drawn towards multidisciplinary studies. Is this a worrying situation? And how are we to make the best of it?

English is a naturally associative subject, in the obvious sense that any work of literature both is something and is about something. The former emphasis will locate *Paradise Lost* in a 'seventeenth-century poetry' context, while the latter can relate it to history or theology. By extension a given individual course can be made the equivalent of the crossword square that links words DOWN and ACROSS. Eighteenth-century literature, is a typical component of an English degree and offers obvious internal cross-connections. But Fielding is arguably closer to Hogarth than to Defoe, Sterne closer to Locke than to Smollett. Both can be of interest to the theologian. The student of Pope will profit from a knowledge of Augustan architecture and landscape gardening. The text of *The Beggar's Opera* can't usefully be studied in isolation from the music. Most of the major writers of the period were enmeshed in its political life. If the course points forwards and backwards to a literary tradition, it points outwards in the direction of several other disciplines—in fact it suggests the possibility of a whole degree in Eighteenth-Century Studies.

Further examples of this sort are easy to improvise. A programme on Modernism could offer connections with History, Art History, Music, Drama, French Literature. A Victorian Studies syllabus could put Hardy alongside Darwin, Tennyson alongside the Pre-Raphaelites. Such cross-disciplinary packages could well be made at least as coherent and intellectually challenging as the traditional English degree. They could prompt creative dialogue between teachers from the several subjects concerned, and redefine research interests.

To lower the tone of the argument, as one currently must: they could also be put together on the cheap. Degrees of this kind can be constructed from units already on offer. A potentially exciting initiative can be pursued at no expense, and without encroachment on existing programmes. Courses under threat because undersubscribed could well be retrieved if thus made to contribute to two degrees rather than one. Many a dwindling department, no longer able to mount a full degree of its own, might be sustained by absorption into programmes of this kind. Student demand for English is currently buoyant, so this is an argument from altruism—but a self-interested altruism in the sense that the loss of any discipline from a university diminishes those that survive. On first thoughts this would seem to be a rare case in which bread-and-butter self-interest and respectable academic experimentation go hand in hand.

A glance through *University Entrance: the Official Guide* might suggest that the point was taken some considerable time ago. In practice we have already conceded that English Literature is divisible. Virtually every university that offers it as a single discipline offers it also in combination with one or more other disciplines. It can be read alongside subjects as diverse as Biology, Maths, Geography, Law, Hebrew, Chinese, Archaeology, Music, and Physical Education. Over a hundred such pairings are available across the British university system. Prospective undergraduates who consult *University Entrance* will conclude that English can go with pretty well anything.

And yet this ostensible plurality is actually a cause for concern. The models I was proposing above involved the cross-relationships of interdisciplinary study. Ideally a programme of that sort, a limited or even prescribed set of courses, is the responsibility of an established panel of teachers, and features at least one bridge-course. It has been made coherent at the cost of hard work.

*Multi*disciplinary degrees, by contrast, can, and often do, come very easily indeed as far as the teachers are concerned: six of one discipline and half-a-dozen of the other, no bridge-course and perhaps very little advice about course choice. Fortunately there is quite a range of possibilities between this *laissez-faire* multidisciplinary worst case, and the interdisciplinary best case. A system of exclusions, pairings and prerequisites can offer intending students a variety of sensible routes through the long, diverse course-lists. Personal academic advice can also be provided, responsive to particular tastes and needs. Careful supervision of both the programme at large and the individual student can redeem the multidisciplinary degree from miscellaneousness.

### III

It is unfortunate but inescapable that the subject of interdisciplinary studies can't usefully be pursued, in present economic circumstances, without this shuttling between academic and financial considerations. Ultimately—and painfully—the two kinds of argument intersect. In this section, however, I'll stick to some of the academic pros and cons.

Personal experience suggests to me that a substantial number of English academics are suspicious of multidisciplinary degrees, or even hostile to them. One version of the 'conservative' or monodisciplinary case would go something like this. The weaker the literary grounding our students have acquired at school, the less will they be equipped to make sense of Milton or Pope *at all*. For them an attempt to link *Paradise Lost* with the Civil War would connect nothing with nothing. By contrast the sequence of literary courses that a single-honours programme offers will cumulatively inculcate linguistic and interpretative skills that at any rate teach the undergraduate how to *read*. Interdisciplinary study only makes sense at postgraduate level, when students will have such skills to work with and from.

Some would push the argument further. With a few exceptions (the claim goes) lecturers in English Literature are not equipped to sidestep into History or Philosophy or whatever. No academic discipline can be casually mastered. Such qualifications as we can claim to possess have been derived from prolonged study of our own discipline: outside it we are amateurs. The same would be true for our potential collaborators in any joint-honours programme. They would do their bit, we would do ours. It would be left to the students to achieve a synthesis that lies beyond the capabilities of their instructors. Only in those rare cases where a group of academics with genuine and related interdisciplinary interests happens to come together is there a possibility of anything more coherent. Let such devise programmes framed to their peculiar abilities and truly collaborative. Only then, with an appropriate apparatus of bridge-courses and joint teaching, might it be remotely possible to squeeze an academic quart into an undergraduate pint pot.

Even this ideal arrangement, however, would not win universal approval in university English departments. The ultimate objection is conceptual. A typical title for such a course, as suggested above, might be Eighteenth-Century Studies or Studies in Modernism. For purists the plural term 'studies' is a confession of incoherence, of miscellaneousness. How could the heterogeneous elements of the programme inculcate a *discipline*? What could such a discipline consist in? *A fortiori* the unstructured English-plus-*X* degree would be still less defensible. A discipline implies and generates a syllabus. The syllabus defines the discipline. No *ad hoc* syllabus can have this defining force.

The most obvious counter-argument is basic and pragmatic. Purist objections of this sort prove too much and come too late. They would apply to any sort of multidisciplinary programme whatever. But joint-degrees featuring English Literature are already on offer throughout our university system. Surely we wouldn't participate in them if we didn't believe in them? We are already committed, as our prospectuses proclaim.

More fundamentally, the purist puts a weight of confidence on certain academic habits and conventions that they cannot be guaranteed to sustain. Although we have a few ancient foundations in the United Kingdom—mostly in Scotland—our university system is largely a product of the last hundred years and has developed uncertainly, by fits and starts. It only *feels*—or used to feel—antique and organic. Within that system few of the seemingly well-established disciplines have much of a pedigree. Many academics resist that thought because it is more reassuring to feel that one is associated with a mature, deep-rooted enterprise. As a result, a newly conceived degree programme that manages to survive the initial hostilities and gain admission to the prospectus swiftly acquires a patina of confidence and pseudo-longevity. If Mods can go with Greats, P and P can bed down with E. When European Studies became a fashionable subject a few years ago, the title at first seemed too absurdly comprehensive to be anything but a joke. A step or two further and we could have had World Studies, which would presumably have given total freedom of manoeuvre. But with degree courses, as with children, the conferring of a name is no more than a speculative, and pretty hopeless, preliminary attempt at definition. The name itself is gradually redefined by the emerging personality. In an academic context European Studies soon ceased to appear an *omnium gatherum* and acquired a meaning in . one sense sufficiently precise. When the subject is discussed in Faculty or Senate we know what range of intellectual activities we are likely to be talking about.

Even if all this is admitted, purist doubts of a conceptual kind may persist. Is the title European Studies more than a flag of convenience? Will the courses studied under this heading be interrelated and mutually supportive? Again, does the syllabus represent a *discipline*?

In this case and in others like it the obvious defensive response is to point out various ways in which the individual courses concerned do hang together, do contribute to a single end. A period 'Studies' degree, for example, could be claimed to teach undergraduates to 'read' an age, or the culture within that age, in much the same way as a literary degree shows them how to read texts.

If, however, these positive arguments fell on deaf ears it wouldn't be difficult for the beleaguered subject to resort to a potentially damaging counter-attack. Certainly the English literature purist who lobs stones at multidisciplinary programming should watch out for flying glass.

For our own discipline is hardly susceptible to strict definition. It can't go demonstrably wrong, in the sense that ill-trained graduates won't be responsible for collapsing bridges or deaths in the operating theatre. There is therefore no external professional body to draw up guidelines and impose standards. Nor have leading exponents of the subject been notable for their ability to achieve consensus about its rationale. There have been vigorous, not to say spiteful, battles about this over the years. In practice the general bias is probably still historical: if a department is fortunate enough to be recruiting a new lecturer, it is likely to advertise for, say, a medieval specialist, or an eighteenth-century specialist. But the specification may mean no more than that certain courses mounted by that department are chronologically defined. Whether complete historical coverage is aimed for, whether certain other courses are linguistic or comparative or theoretical, whether genre is studied, whether the degree includes an element of American literature—all these questions and many others are still open.

In theory this could be a perfectly healthy state of affairs. Different departments could choose to go in different, but equally respectable, directions. In practice, and for a variety of reasons, the picture is more confused than that. Young academics seeking for a university English post could hardly restrict themselves to departments whose syllabuses they wholeheartedly approved. They got in where they could. Many, if not most, of our English departments are accordingly divided on questions of course-structure, methodology, fundamental purpose. If all our university teachers of English could assemble at some great conference that would enable the like-minded to group together to devise new departments the problem could be solved (at least temporarily): we could indeed offer a wide variety of different, distinctly defined, English syllabuses. But this can't and won't happen, so our departments remain potentially fractious.

A redeeming factor, mentioned earlier, is the shared confidence in the integrity and usefulness of the individual course. Lecturers will not be too disgruntled about a course-structure they disapprove of, as long as they are left free to teach in their own way those well-tried seminars on *Macbeth* or 'Michael' or *Middlemarch*. But (to repeat) might not such a unit fit just as meaningfully into a degree-programme in Renaissance or Romantic or Victorian Studies?

## IV

Sadly in the present economic situation the arguments for flexibility can't be considered merely on their academic merits, because they could push the academic study of English literature to the brink of a very slippery slope. I've been suggesting that in theory, at least, the syllabus defines the discipline, or the discipline as locally understood. It also defines the department. If the syllabus unfurls and various courses are seen as detachable, the department may suffer a dangerous loss of definition.

The context in which this threat could be crucial is the now commonplace situation in which a head of department has to argue for the replacement of an academic who has retired or died. In most British universities nowadays the only argument that stands a chance of succeeding is the argument from indispensability—and this can be a difficult card to play. The claim 'We must replace Dr Smith, because he was our only medievalist' won't carry much weight unless the sentence can continue: '. . . and medieval literature has always been an intrinsic part of our syllabus'.

Even this claim leaves the department open to a Vice-Chancellor's knight's fork. Should he refuse to replace Dr Smith, either the degree-programme must be cut back and restructured or Dr Jones, who took a couple of medieval papers as an undergraduate, must bone up and take over. If the programme is cut back once, it can be cut back again. Next time the victim might be Jacobean Drama or American Literature. Don't departments elsewhere make do without such courses? If on the other hand Dr Jones proves adaptable to the required extent, his colleagues may be expected to do likewise. One of *them* can be pushed sideways into Jacobean Drama or American Literature. Such moves have been widespread over the past few years and have undoubtedly served to weaken the notion of specialisation within the discipline.

But if the shrinking department cannot even make the kind of claim suggested above, the case is still worse. Its English Literature degree might seem to mean no more than a nosegay of eight courses selected from a larger bunch proffered by the handbook. At an extreme the department as such would lose its purpose. If all that the university requires of it is the capacity to mount a range of courses sufficiently numerous and sufficiently various, the obvious economy is to resort more and more to part-time teachers, paid at hourly rates.

Too casual an involvement in joint-honours degrees is a step towards conceding the vital point. Will the individual course, however worthy in itself, look like an integral component of a coherent single-honours degree, when it can be taken along with any other three English courses in combination with four courses from any one of a dozen other disciplines? The abstract issue quickly becomes distinct in practice. It is one thing to discuss the *Lyrical Ballads* with a group of single-honours students who have read some Pope and Milton, another to elucidate them to a seminar consisting of joint-honours students in Drama, Computing, History and Sociology, a junior-year student from California and short-stay visitors from Tokyo and Turin. This doesn't mean that the latter activity isn't worth while, but it represents a different kind of work—and one that hasn't traditionally been associated with our universities.

If all our individual courses may be detached and relocated in this way, what, if anything, can be said to be intrinsic to the single-honours English degree? In my own department, less than twenty years ago, a professor argued strenuously that it was unthinkable that a student should graduate in English without having read some Spenser. A decade later another member of the department was making much the same case on behalf of Milton. Within the last couple of years we have debated whether the Shakespeare course should remain compulsory. The discussions concerned were all reasonable: in each case the suggestion had been that a given element of the degree should cease to be compulsory in the interests of giving the students greater freedom to construct their own programmes. My point is that for the sake of this flexibility and wider choice we were whittling away the common denominators in our syllabus. We may have been right to do so, but one of the risks we have taken is that *all* our courses might now be regarded as provisional and therefore as detachable or replaceable.

It may be objected that this problem is hardly unique to English, or to the humanities: all academic disciplines not defined by a set of professional requirements are vulnerable to the same sort of objection, or to some version of it. But the case isn't likely to be made against subjects now in political favour as being 'relevant'. Moreover a discipline is far less vulnerable when it demands prior qualifications and works incrementally. By contrast, any fluent reader of English could, at least in theory, attend the seminar on *Macbeth* or 'Michael' or *Middlemarch*. It is this consideration that puts us in a weak position. If students become still more inclined to go for a 'careers' element in a joint-honours degree, many of the courses we offer may come to seem no more than the academic jam on their vocational bread and butter. As the financial strings are pulled tighter, we may increasingly be called upon to put on special seminars for visiting foreign students, or mount money-making summer-schools for the general public.

V

I hinted at the outset that my arguments would pull in different directions. My own position, for what it's worth, is that while interdisciplinary study can be not only respectable but exciting and creative—though it often isn't—pursuit of it in the current climate might, unless we are careful, seriously undermine English Literature as a university discipline.

'The current climate' and 'the economic situation' are miserable phrases to have to revert to in the course of what a few years ago would have been a purely intellectual or pedagogic argument. The emphasis must seem irritating and demeaning to readers in other countries. In relation to interdisciplinary study, however, it does seem to me that this sense of exigency eventually poses an academic challenge of a serious and interesting kind. I would like to conclude by developing this point.

I say 'eventually': there are several preceding phases. In the first, now long past, universities and departments could usefully prune excesses, financial or academic. In a second phase, degree courses, and indeed activities of all kinds, are cut back beyond reasonable limits, and impaired. In a third—the phase I've been principally concerned with in this chapter—the search for further savings is so desperate that valued traditions and conventions are abandoned, to be supplanted by a variety of *ad hoc* arrangements. The academic machine is overhauled and taken to pieces so often as to suggest that it is indeed no more than an assemblage of cogs—that there is no lurking ghost. This is a reductive and demoralising phase. A department that has been cut by a third or perhaps even by half cannot, even in conceptual terms, be seen as the thing it was.

But the arguments for interdisciplinarity are arguments for seeing the diminished department as something else—something of equal value. The individual course and the degree-programme that hold together through cross-relationship and mutual reinforcement mimic the very structure of the faculty or the university. If the academic's first reaction, when under threat, is to seek refuge in the definitions and conventions of his own discipline, a second and more hopeful one might be to look to a wider academic tradition, a stronger sense of intellectual fraternity with other subjects.

At the practical level this development can't come easily. Universities have been heavily compartmentalised. Since most university teachers have had a specialised academic training, amounting to a sort of tunnel vision, it's hardly surprising that we're short of colliery managers. For years there has been a division between departmental decisions that were scrupulously, even over-scrupulously, debated, and interdepartmental decisions that tended to be taken in a loosely permissive spirit. Perhaps for this reason our university system can offer such a huge menu of interdisciplinary degrees. All that was necessary formally to create most of them would have been a motion to Senate that subject *A* could henceforth be combined with subject *B*. There need not have been any theoretical discussion or allocation of responsibility for the new programmes. It is symptomatic that in many faculties the results of the finals papers of the single-honours student will be collectively and carefully analysed within one meeting, while those of the multidisciplinary candidate will be more cursorily reviewed over a couple of briefer sittings.

If it is hard to run an efficient interdisciplinary programme, it is doubly hard to devise the administrative and organisational structures that would facilitate doing so. Courses in the various component disciplines must be made all of the same length, so that there is a common unit of exchange. Prospectuses and handbooks must be restructured and rewritten. Complex timetabling problems must be solved, concerning both courses and examinations. New kinds of cross-departmental committee must be formed. All this in face of the natural tendency of the academic mind to accept and in some sense sentimentalise the status quo while producing all sorts of ingenious objections to any proposed innovation.

But such efforts are worthwhile. Indeed, in this period of apparent scepticism about the value of higher education as we have known it, they are essential. To pursue in these practical terms the ideal of interdisciplinary study is to demonstrate a continuing belief in the idea of the university.

# English across the Binary Line: An Institutional View

## DANIEL LAMONT

The year 1988 brought in major changes to the funding and governance of both universities and Public Sector Higher Education institutions—now to be called the Polytechnic and Colleges sector— following the passage of the Education Reform Act. At the same time a variety of methods for funding higher education are under discussion and the introduction of student loans has now been formally proposed by the Government. Simultaneous with these changes, there is a renewed questioning of what should be taught in higher education. Everything has been shaken up and its future shape is hard to predict.

There is a clear demand for accountability, and performance indicators are now required as one essential means of providing that accountability. One such is the employment rate of graduands from different courses as a measure of the utility of courses. There is a view, held particularly by the Treasury, that higher education must serve the needs of the economy and that it 'really' must be more vocational and oriented towards training, rather than towards liberal notions of education. Thus, there has been a developing hostility towards supposedly non-functional subjects: sociology has long been the bugbear of the right, largely because it is seen as subversive, but this suspicion is increasingly directed at humanities and social science courses generally. This is despite the fact that manpower planning is a notoriously uncertain art and that 40 per cent of all jobs advertised are non-subject specific. None the less, there is a marked preference for the applied sciences, computing and business and management studies at the expense of the humanities. Yet, ironically there is a shortage of good candidates for engineering subjects while English is very popular with prospective students. Another performance indicator is the cost of operating courses. On this yardstick, English is a desirable subject because its degree courses are inexpensive to run and there is a large market for it. (Oh! how easy it is, these days, to slip into commercial jargon!)

Thus English may seem to be beleaguered on both sides of the binary line and recent suggestions that business and industry should contribute substantially to the funding of higher education may reinforce anxieties, for they are not likely to support the humanities. Yet in the same speech as the Secretary of State for Education, Mr Kenneth Baker, calls for increased financial involvement by business, he also calls for an improvement in access so that the participation rate in higher education will double from its present 15 per cent to 30 per cent by the year 2014. Such an expansion should benefit English. The whole of Mr Baker's speech, given at Lancaster University in January 1989, repays study but the following extract illustrates not only the possibilities but also the anxieties he raises:

> In my view, the pursuit of knowledge as an object of interest in and for itself remains the cornerstone of the whole higher education edifice. But knowledge for its own sake is not and has never been the only value of importance in higher education. Alongside the disinterested pursuit of knowledge, feeding off it, and also vitalizing it, 'vocationalism' has always had its place in higher education—which has always performed an important service function. All of this means that we shall have to be careful not to generalize about 'quality', on the basis of traditions of cultural exclusiveness which belonged to the world of three per cent partici-pation in higher education and which are neither appropriate nor sustainable in a world of 30 per cent participation.[1]

While it is good that the value of the disinterested pursuit of knowledge is recognised, what priority does it have in relation to 'vocationalism' and just what is the point being made about 'quality'?

There is a tendency in some quarters to see the polytechnics and colleges as being in a quite different situation from the universities, with the humanities being more securely entrenched in the latter. I am not so sure. The phasing out of Music at Aberdeen University or Philosophy at Newcastle University represents the increasing vulner-ability of the humanities in universities. To the outsider, the dis-tinction between the polytechnics and the universities is hard to grasp: both systems award degrees, undergraduate and graduate, both are of a comparable size, and with the exception of medicine and dentistry both offer a similar range of subjects. (The nearest analogy is to be found in the USA where the 'State' and the 'private' universities exist alongside each other.) Of course there are distinctions and differences but both systems are concerned with higher education, educating students to a comparable standard, ensured by the use of external examiners. My own view is that the old practice of suspicion and

assumption of superiority between the two sectors is no longer justified. It is above all not to be justified between the two sets of
humanities. (It is, happily, less often encountered but it still exists.)
There is much in common and the problems to be confronted are the
same. This is not to say that there is—or should be—uniformity of
practice but the similarities are stronger than the differences. The loss,
contraction or threat to any part of the humanities, in whatever part of
the higher education system, diminishes us all, not simply the teachers
and scholars in the profession of English but society at large. This is
not to argue against necessary change but to argue that it is futile and
dishonest to take comfort in the perception, not uncommon, that there
might be other departments and institutions which could act as a
shield against cuts. The threat to 'economise' English affects us all.
Moreover, as I argue later, I think that in ten years' time the binary
line will have either vanished or have been so eroded as to be
meaningless.

In the past twenty-five years, the polytechnics and colleges have
developed an impressive and diverse range of courses in the
humanities in general and in English in particular. The process has
been an interesting one. Most of the institutions placed a·heavy
emphasis on technical and business subjects, usually with an applied
bent. Some had always maintained work in the humanities and social
studies—often teaching external London University degrees but also
providing the 'broadening' elements of communications or liberal
studies as part of business and technological courses. In the 1970s, this
was reinforced by a number of mergers between colleges, as colleges of
education were amalgamated, often with polytechnics. As English was
always central to teacher education, this series of amalgamations
tended to strengthen English teaching groups. The original architects
of the polytechnics and colleges apparently saw these institutions as
being vocationally oriented and did not consciously intend that they
should develop a substantial portfolio of work in the humanities. This
differs from the new universities founded in the 1960s which did set
out from the beginning to develop work in all areas of knowledge,
including the humanities. Polytechnics may have had mixed feelings
towards English but, apart from the intrinsic worth of the subject,
their directors seem to have recognised that English was not a costly
subject to run and that it was very popular and attracted a large
number of students to their institutions. I also sense that recently
polytechnics have wanted to be more diverse and 'balanced' institutions than seemed to be the case on designation in the period

1968–1972.[2] Whatever the motives, by the time the National Advisory Body (NAB) was set up in 1982, English and the other humanities subjects were well established and were thus incorporated into the planning system. That system did impose limits on student numbers but these have not been as stringent as it might appear, since some overrun of recruitment targets was permitted. In 1986, it is true, NAB did propose to close certain English courses—also courses in Engineering and other favoured areas—but these proposals were successfully resisted. What will happen under the PCFC (Polytechnics and Colleges Funding Council) regime in the future remains to be seen. That body is still establishing its processes and procedures.

The establishment of English in the public sector did not mean that these new English degree courses necessarily followed those patterns set by university courses. The course development process gave every one the opportunity to begin afresh, rather than struggle with existing structures and practices. Inevitably, teaching staff reacted to the kind of undergraduate education that they themselves had received, rejecting some aspects but retaining others.

Educationally, the process of validation has had a striking effect. With few exceptions, the polytechnics had their courses validated by the Council for National Academic Awards (CNAA). The council established a procedure: submission documents were prepared in which the course team elaborated in some detail their syllabus proposals in the context of the degree scheme as a whole. This forced them to go back to first principles and look hard at their basic aims and objectives rather than accept traditional practices as given, not to be questioned. The procedure also forced the development of the subject team. The teachers of the subject were expected to function not as a series of individuals but as a group of people who had collectively put together an integrated degree scheme after much discussion and debate. There was stress on coherence both in the teaching and in the curriculum. This group solidarity was reinforced by the validation event itself. A panel of members of the appropriate subject board would visit the institution for what were rather euphemistically called 'discussions' but which in the early days tended to be aggressively conducted adversarial sessions, perhaps especially so when sometimes the visitors came from local and possibly rival institutions. No matter what the style of the event might be, the arrival of a group of outsiders with power to allow or disallow a course proposal was bound to engender a strong sense of group solidarity on the part of the proposing team. Nor is all finished when the course is approved: every five years there is a progress review when a critical appraisal of the course is demanded, with the assumption that some changes will be made.

The process outlined here may seem cumbersome and bureaucratic but it has been enormously beneficial. The ostensible purpose of the exercise was to ensure that the degree teaching was of an appropriate standard and comparable with that in the universities. The secondary effect was to question the very nature of a subject, here English, in a creative way. As John Oakley and Elizabeth Owen have remarked:

> . . . the pressure to write is itself the source of a modest critical defamiliarization in most of us and, where we are working with others, of a greater self-consciousness about our ideas and the way in which they differ from those of other people. It is, on the whole, a very different process of validation and development than that followed in the universities.[3]

This context within which English has developed has meant that English in the public sector has its own character. In only four polytechnics does English exist as a separate department or school. The pattern is that English as a division or section within a larger department, with a name such as Humanities or Language and Literature, which is itself located in a faculty. This structure has made it very difficult for English to remain isolated from other humanities subjects. It has become natural for them to work closely together. In the early days resource and staffing constraints forced some institutions to build degree course teams round a number of subjects. The consequence, together with the rethinking that the validation process called for, has been that in the public sector English is overwhelmingly taught as a component of a large multi-subject degree, usually comprising other humanities and social science subjects. Indeed, in at least two institutions it is possible to take English alongside science or business subjects as well. The introduction of modular or credit-accumulation schemes can only facilitate this. English, therefore, firmly exists in a multidisciplinary framework and is often taught in an interdisciplinary way. This insists on the student taking a broader view than the traditional single-honours degree requires. In fact in 1986 a survey revealed that there were only seven single-honours degrees in English in the public sector. Clearly, the context of English has had an inevitable effect on its content.

Hitherto, I suspect that there has been a greater diversity of students in the polytechnics than in the universities—drawn not only from widely differing age-ranges but also from a wide variety of experiences and backgrounds. A very high proportion of such students are older students, returning to education after a long gap, usually without the standard entry qualifications. Institutions have developed access courses to encourage re-entry. Some have established innovative schemes whereby parts of courses have been 'franchised' to other colleges in the region. Fundamental to this widening of opportunity is the development of part-time degree routes which may be daytime only or, increasingly, offered in the evening. In my own institution, Lancashire Polytechnic, the distinction between evening and daytime students is being eroded since certain course units are only offered in the evening, to be taken by full and part-time students alike. Polytechnics are usually city-centre institutions and this accessibility, together with their long tradition of part-time teaching, has made them very attractive to part-time students. With this clientele, English is a very popular subject. The new flexible approaches to study lend themselves to English degree courses more than most others. I am sure, therefore, that the newly found wish to increase the participation rate in higher education, partly by drawing in new kinds of student studying other than full-time for three years, will strengthen English on both sides of the binary line. These non-traditional students may be demanding to teach but they are also often extremely rewarding. Many of them do well despite not having the normal qualifications and the success of the Open University is most instructive in this respect. The effect of the introduction of student loans is unpredictable at present but could well be a disincentive to prospective students. However, the availability of different modes of study allied to the inherent attractiveness of our subject should secure its continuance. It is noteworthy that, in the public sector, taught MA degrees in the humanities are becoming more common. Significantly, they are almost always part-time, only available in the evenings. This not only reflects the extreme scarcity of support for the postgraduate student in the humanities but also caters for those students who do not want to or simply cannot study full-time. In the new climate, English may be better placed to survive than many think if it does not insist on following traditional patterns of study.

The environment within which public sector institutions operate has changed entirely within the past two years and they have now achieved a great deal of autonomy. Firstly, the CNAA has drawn back from its customary role of external and superior controller of academic quality to adopt more of a monitoring role. Increasingly, it has tended to work in partnership with institutions. In 1987–88 it embarked on a process of accreditation whereby large and experienced institutions were invited to demonstrate their ability to operate their own internal systems of validation and review (using external specialists). Most polytechnics were successful. Their degrees are now awarded by their own academic boards and thus they have now achieved an academic autonomy very similar to that enjoyed by the universities. CNAA is a slimmed-down and much less powerful body. Who knows, it may even wither away with time.

This process is parallel to the achievement of administrative autonomy. The Education Reform Act of 1988 has separated polytechnics and colleges from the control of local authorities and they are now independent corporations. Their new governing bodies are smaller, dominated by members drawn from local business, industry and professions who supply the chair, and with very limited representation of either staff or local authorities. They are no longer to be seen simply as local authority institutions. The directors and governing bodies have been given very large powers, including 'the determination of the educational character' and mission of their institutions. Indeed the director is to be thought of as the Chief Executive Officer: a title more commonly found in large companies than in higher education. Academic boards are reduced in size, thus becoming less representative, and have fewer powers, thus becoming largely advisory. Polytechnics and colleges are now autonomous, but have little collegiality, although it is true that the democratic spirit was always more apparent than real. The distinction between charitable status and company status of the reconstituted institutions is significant. To see 'and partners' after the name of a college—there is already one example—chills the spirit. However, the need to make money by the selling of services and skills in the market place will mean that a trading arm will have to be set up. I am sure that universities too will become more autocratically and managerially run institutions: indeed that is the intended consequence of the Jarrett Report.

As these changes settle down, it will become clear that to have a higher education system consisting of two broadly comparable sectors, each with a funding council, each made up of autonomous institutions with similar, if not identical objectives, will begin to look absurd. The proposal to change the practice of funding universities on the basis that 40 per cent of the time of all academic staff is spent on research in favour of providing a basic allocation for teaching, leaving universities or individual departments themselves to bid for research allocations, will put them in a similar position to that of the polytechnics. The case for maintaining two separate systems will be eroded. Some institutions on both sides of the binary line may not survive the new dispensation. They will either close or merge, and there is no reason why these mergers should not cross the binary line. Another possibility is the emergence of regional federations of higher education institutions: there is already an example in the Welsh universities.

A report on English in the universities based on questionnaires circulated to heads of department in late 1987[4] records a major loss of teaching staff with some 148 posts disappearing between January 1981 and September 1987. In general there was little hope of improvement. This has meant a sacrifice of specialist teaching and expertise. Thus the range of courses available to students is reduced; in particular, newly developed areas such as Women and Literature or Literary Theory have been damaged. Clearly the richness and variety of courses of study in English have been greatly curtailed. The effect of the closure of other Arts departments has also led to the loss of certain joint degree courses. Postgraduate work is constrained. Library expenditure, especially on the Arts, and, within that, especially on periodicals, has been drastically reduced. There has, too, been restructuring so that cognate departments are now linked together to form schools. Staff have had to spend more time on administration and have had less time for teaching and scholarship. Research activity has been cut back. Evidence of the deleterious effect of the cutbacks is clear.

I read the report with a sense of *déjà vu*. The survey carried out by SCEPSHE in 1986 revealed a very similar picture.[5] The difference lies in the starting point. Public sector teaching staff have always carried high teaching and administrative loads, and sabbatical leave has been practically unknown. The whole question of research and scholarship is an ambiguous one. The universities have always emphasised research and expected evidence of this from publication—although the value of the latter as a performance indicator of anything other than industry may be debatable. The polytechnics have always seen themselves primarily as teaching institutions: that has not prevented a great deal of research from being carried out and more space must be found for it. However, we would all agree that undergraduate teaching must be firmly grounded in scholarship; in the keeping up to date in developments in the subject area and being sensitive to new possibilities and interests. The space for this essential scholarly activity has been squeezed very badly. Public sector staff are overly pressed and are somewhat demoralised. There was never a 'golden age' for English in the public sector, when the subject expanded rapidly, as in the 1960s in the new universities. Developments have always been carried out on a shoestring. What is amazing is how good and exciting those developments have been. If the proposals mooted to grade universities into three categories were applied to polytechnics, it is by no means certain that all or even most of the latter would fall into the lowest one of 'teaching only' institutions. The polytechnics' research base is a strong one.

We now live in a political regime which lays great stress on the need for 'value for money', for education to be linked to employment and vocation. The Minister of State, Mr Robert Jackson, has invited (instructed?) the universities to leave their 'secret garden'. We are told that we now live in an enterprise culture and money is therefore being directed towards encouraging enterprise in the undergraduate curriculum. There is the sense that perhaps the government wishes to see the public sector as mainly concerned with 'vocational' training. But is not all higher education being pressed to become training rather than education? In such a world, the tenure of English and its sister arts might seem precarious. It is seen to be irrelevant and unproductive. Yet, paradoxically, if market forces really did obtain, we would expand, not restrict, opportunities for the study of English. There are large numbers of prospective students for our subject and it is not expensive to run. By contrast, science and technology courses are very expensive to operate and have difficulty in attracting sufficient students. English is quite as vocational and relevant as many other subjects. Its 'transferable skills' are just as good as those of many more obviously utilitarian disciplines.

Without being unduly defensive, I think we must ask what English is for and indeed what English is. John Daniel in his introduction to *English in the Public Sector: The Current Debate* remarks:

> There seem to be two main fronts where it is necessary for English to define itself at the present time. One is outwards towards a model of society in which government proposals appear to take on an ever-more reductive view of the Arts and Humanities. The other is inwards, towards an examination of English in its traditional institutional formation with its conventional syllabus and isolation from other disciplines.[6]

I have in this essay offered some discussion of English in its institutional formation, especially within the public sector. I have suggested that there, it does not really exist in isolation from other disciplines but works closely with them. This context has forced a reappraisal of the subject which has led to changes.

Part of the difficulty in the current debate about the nature of our subject is that 'English' as a label is ambiguous if not misleading. To many outside—and this includes many within our own institutions—English is seen to relate to English language work, as it usually does in schools, or English as a second language. At worst it is thought of as the teaching of memo and report writing, i.e. a basic literacy. On the other hand, English to most of us within is a shorthand for English Literature, the study of literary texts. That view is too restrictive. At least the Scottish university where I did my own undergraduate degree called the degree course English Language and Literature. That in itself was curious since much of the language and literature we studied was in fact Scottish, not English, and was written in Scots. Again there is a curious ambiguity about the label 'English Language'. Very often it refers to the study of the history of the English language, in one form an old fashioned philology and the study of pre-Chaucerian texts, not all of which are necessarily literary. (It is odd that the very people who happily accept the study of Old or Middle English chronicles often object to the literary study of more recent historical narratives.) Linguistics in this country may well have connections with the study of foreign languages but it is overwhelmingly concerned with the study of the English language. One may, therefore, find a university with a department of English Language and Literature and a separate department of Linguistics and Modern English Literature. There may be pragmatic and historical reasons for all this, but the resultant confusion is unhelpful.

It would be much more satisfactory if we could see English—with its values and resonances of heritage so much in tune with the current Government's thinking—as being an overarching label.

Within it clearly lie the areas of Literary Studies, a title I prefer to English Literature, and also of Language Studies which must include some linguistics. Since I also think that students should have some nodding acquaintance with theory, linguistics will contribute to that. Within this broad area of English I would also include work in Cultural Studies and Communications Studies, which demand links with History and other social sciences. For myself, working with colleagues from both History and Geography on an interdisciplinary course in American Culture and Society has been most fruitful. We live in an age where the printed book is no longer the central fact of our culture. If people do read novels, they are as likely to read Jackie Collins, Arthur Hailey or Jeffrey Archer as Jane Austen or James Joyce. They are even more likely to watch television. These phenomena must be subjected to rigorous critical analysis. The appropriate umbrella is English but that is not to suggest that they are the same as *Middlemarch* or 'The Waste Land': I do not say that there are no distinctions, either of value or of kind, to be drawn between these works.

The context of English in the public sector, its place in the institutional structure, and the course development and validation process it has undergone have opened up our concept of what English might be. This had led to changes in what has been taught under this label and this process has to be related to recent debates on a theoretical level. There is a greater variety in what is available to students in the public sector than in the universities. Within English, there are a number of legitimate possibilities but the one requirement that I would make is that all students should do some work on modern English language.

It has been suggested that English in the public sector is simply discourse analysis under another name and that there is a general hostility to works of the imagination. This is not the case. There is still ample opportunity for the study of literature in the traditional way. Those of us who are teachers of literature are open to the creative and imaginative resonances of the texts that we teach and we hope that our students respond to those resonances too. We also hope that we have conveyed to the student a capacity to reflect not only on the texts themselves but also on their process of reading them. So yes, 'traditional' English is still available. On the other hand, there is also available a variety of activities under the heading 'English' other than the specifically literary. This pluralism is surely most desirable, and students do not necessarily have to make absolute choices. It is also educationally healthy that students are required to study at least one other subject. The combination of English with other cognate subjects such as History, History of Art, Linguistics or foreign languages is enriching for both the two subjects and the student him/herself. Moreover, since I place a high value on the study of English, in whatever its form, I welcome modular degree programmes which enable students to combine subjects such as Mathematics, Law, Computing or a science, for that also is enriching. For too long the model of the single-honours degree has obtained. Too often it has seemed that the purpose of such degrees has simply been to secure the next generation of English academics.

In a political and economic climate which makes the unfettered operation of market forces an article of faith, people in the profession of English inevitably see the subject as falling victim to the new utilitarianism. I am more optimistic. I have argued that the consequence of the recent changes must be to erode to a large extent the distinctions between English in the universities and in the public sector, which are, I have suggested, the product of different histories. Both are now subject to the same forces. I expect that the universities, like the polytechnics, will pursue policies for wider access and develop more part-time courses. This does not mean that the nature of the English taught will necessarily be any more uniform than now, but I do foresee a convergence.

Underlying my assessment has been a reluctance to accept the simple dichotomy between 'disinterested pursuit of knowledge' and vocationalism. In the humane and imaginative terms that I have suggested, English is an eminently practical subject. It is perhaps the most entrepreneurial of all subjects. It draws on a variety of intellectual pursuits and encourages students to think laterally. The communicative, creative and analytical skills that our students require make them highly employable. It is interesting that in some North American quarters the appropriateness of the humanities as part of a business education has now been recognised. None of this need devalue the intrinsic quality of the subject. In its various forms English provides a liberal education in the way it develops and empowers the individual student. The case for English can be made but it must be done collaboratively, not competitively, across the binary line.

## Notes

1 'Baker's Vision for the Next 25 Years', *The Times Higher Education Supplement*, 13 January, 1989 No. 845 p. 7

2 For instance, Lancashire Polytechnic's Mission Statement includes as an aim that it wishes to 'provide the widest possible scope, choice and flexibility in its educational activities and facilities to meet the demands of those individuals who seek to benefit from them'.

3 John Oakley and Elizabeth Owen 'English and the Council for National Academic Awards', in Peter Widdowson (ed) *Re-reading English* (1982) p. 111. This is a very illuminating collection of essays, very relevant to my discussion. It aroused some controversy which is interestingly analysed in Tony Davies

'Damning the Tides: The New English and Reviewers' in M. Green and R. Hoggart (ed) *Broadening the Context* (1987).

[4] Survey carried out by the Committee for University English 1988.

[5] Survey carried out by the Standing Conference on English Higher Education (SCEPSHE), 1986.

[6] John Daniel (ed) *English in the Public Sector: The Current Debate* published by the Standing Conference on English in the Public Sector Higher Education. Copies obtainable from D. R. Lamont at Lancashire Polytechnic, Preston PRI 2TQ.

# English Departments in British Higher Education: A view from Abroad

## ROGER D. SELL

Born and bred in England, I read English at Oxford and went on to do a B. Litt. Since then I have been in frequent contact with English departments in the UK, but have mainly lived abroad, especially in Sweden and in Finland, where I took my doctorate. My personal history will of course influence what follows here, but to some extent I shall also be describing the views of other English scholars in Scandinavia and mainland Europe.[1]

English departments in Britain and English departments on the continent work within two entirely different educational contexts. In Britain, a relatively low proportion of the population enters higher education, and competition for places in English can be stiff: Finnish and Spanish English departments cream off applicants with an entrance examination, but elsewhere on the continent a respectable performance in the school-leaving examination is the only prerequisite for registration, which means that in France and Italy, for instance, first-year courses are hopelessly overcrowded. In Britain, there is throughout an extremely favourable staff–student ratio, and tutorials have an important place: Finnish English departments give about 20 per cent of their teaching to groups of five or less, but elsewhere groups are all much larger, and several countries rely almost exclusively on lectures. British students usually complete their degree studies within three years: Belgium and Holland have fixed time limits (four years and six years), but most continental countries do not, and most students study from four to seven or even ten years, usually finishing with a fairly substantial Master's thesis and often starting families and jobs while still at university. British students are generally expected to sit for examinations and to pass them at first attempt: continental students often take time off or drop out altogether, and they can make repeated attempts at one and the same examination. British students often study only one subject for their degree: in Spain all degrees are of this kind, and in Holland, Norway, Denmark, and Iceland some are, but by far the majority of continental students combine two, three, or even four subjects. British students are expected to do a lot of independent reading and writing: continental students are in some respects more spoon-fed (though in Germany and Switzerland there is an extremely wide range of courses to choose from), and, their proficiency training notwithstanding, they probably write fewer essays than British students overall. Some British students of English become school-teachers, but many enter other professions, and the departmental ethos has much to do with developing individual powers of sensibility, thought and expression: some continental students of English, especially in Denmark, Germany and Holland, now enter other professions, and genuine efforts are made in the direction of a liberal education, but most students still become school-teachers or language experts in business, and departments often seek to justify their activities in terms of vocational training and of increasing the country's competitiveness in international markets.

In different moods one can view these contrasts in different lights. Sometimes British education seems aimed at excellence, strongly interactional, intense, effective, specialised, conducive to independence, and liberal; while continental education seems unambitious, unstimulating, slow, sloppy, superficial, authoritarian, and utilitarian. Or British education seems élitist, insufficiently detached, too quick, overforced, narrow, conducive to idiosyncrasy, and dilettante; while continental education seems democratic, objective, well geared to natural processes of maturation, humanely relaxed, broad-based, conducive to social cohesion, and purposeful.

Though my continental colleagues would not wish to go over to the British system in all its aspects, many of them have very happy memories from their own student days or sabbaticals in British departments. They hope that ERASMUS will make it easier for their undergraduate and postgraduate students to follow in their footsteps and that British host institutions will do even more to facilitate integration with British staff and students, particularly for the visiting research student, who is sometimes left too much to his own devices. They have no wish to send their pupils to Britain for courses aimed at miscellaneous foreigners only, nor really for courses tailor-made for students just from their own country, excellent in their way though the latter can be. What counts most of all is the genuinely British educational experience, shared with British students: its unique intellectual stimulus, the warm friendships cemented during the course of it, the immersion in British life and ways of thought.

They sometimes suspect that from the university teacher's point of view the British system is less than kind, imposing heavy teaching loads and allowing too few opportunities for research. This only makes their admiration for the research accomplished still more heartfelt. They perceive the German tradition of research in English as older, but those of other countries as on the whole younger, and sometimes still undergoing teething troubles, while Britain has produced a steady stream of excellent and fundamental work in nearly all areas.

This is the main reason why they find the cut-backs in British departments so disturbing, but their response is often tinged with rueful fellow-feeling: 'In my country, genetic engineering would have been a better bet,' as somebody has written to me. Out of sheer despondency some have resigned themselves to the adverse climate of opinion; some say that one must try to make a virtue of necessity and to accept the dominant ideology in a more positive spirit; and others say that one should keep up a running battle with it.

A department should not become too fixed in attitudes of either support or opposition *vis à vis* the government of the day—or decade—but also it should not make itself an ivory tower or lose heart. Rather, in both teaching and research it should have goals and standards which no scholar or politician—of whatever colour—will be able to disparage. In this connection, moreover, the coexistence of the British and the continental educational systems begins to look like a source of strength, since each system has tended to preserve and emphasise aspects of English as a subject which have not been so fully developed within the other. Continental scholars, meditating upon Britain, cannot but see ways in which their own departments could do more to bring out the humanistic potential of English. At the same time, they wonder whether some British departments could not have a still sharper sense of their own social responsibility and give even more indication of the subject's wider bearings and significance: another colleague has written that the besetting sin of British departments is actually 'in-group trivialisation of the subject.'

One area in which a leaf could be taken out of each other's book is proficiency training. In continental departments, proficiency is seen as very much a part of what English is about, and often much gruelling effort goes into courses whose only purpose is to train the various skills; the subject-matter on which the skills are developed is not the English language or English literature, but anything under the sun. In Britain, a high level of proficiency is usually taken for granted and is further developed through activities not primarily thought of as proficiency training: discussions and essays about various aspects of English as an academic subject. This contrast, to teachers on both sides of the sea, has long seemed entirely natural, but may reflect only one historical period's wisdom in the matter of language learning.

Although in learning a language foreigners are in a different situation from its native speakers and the mental processes involved also tend to be different, the differences are not all to the native speaker's advantage. As far as the end result is concerned—the skills actually achieved—there are only differences of degree, not kind. The best continental students of English, given a deep immersion in the language and its cultures throughout the long course of their studies, can acquire a very high proficiency level indeed. Recognising this and admiring the 'indirect' proficiency training of British departments, continental scholars may well ask themselves whether their own departments could not take proficiency a little more for granted. *Every* course in English, no matter what else it did, could also be a proficiency course, which would mean there could be fewer proficiency-only courses, necessary though they will remain for some purposes. Synergy would result from developing proficiency on topics that students are really interested in and learning about, and from their having to activate their new knowledge to form arguments. In some departments this is happening already.

By the same token, some British departments are already finding cause to take proficiency rather *less* for granted, both in their own students and in society as a whole. In all modern societies telecommunications are exercising pressures away from literacy towards a new orality and visuality, but in many countries, and especially in Britain, other factors also give food for thought. Britain is a polycultural society, and the divides are not only of race or country of origin but class, so that not even all English native speakers share the same communicative skills. People on the continent have long suspected that the British educational system, or to be precise the existence of more than one educational system in Britain, tends to institutionalise and increase sociocultural divisions, and that to some extent the country wills upon itself its tabloid press, its football hooliganism, its crimerate. They see GCSE, the National Curriculum and the Cox Report as steps in the right direction and will quite understand the reasoning behind a broader acceptance of responsibility by higher education English departments. Among other things, this could be a return to the spirit—if not the detailed practice—of the old Scottish traditions of rhetoric and grammar. Another parallel would be with the composition and rhetoric programmes of American universities. Yet there would probably be more to it than just some direct training of students' proficiency. Greater emphasis could also be given to applied linguistics and sociolinguistics in the wide senses. Graduates, whether they became teachers or politicians or journalists, would then be able to behave with informed attitudes about the nature of language, its capabilities, limitations and roles, and to think clearly on sensitive issues such as the relationship between standard forms of a language and social and regional variants. The English Department of University College London seems to be one of the ones which embrace this mission.[2] Doubtless others will follow suit, becoming more enthusiastically—though not exclusively—*language* departments.

At the moment it would seem that a dominant position in British departments is still held by the discussion of literary texts from Shakespeare to the early twentieth century. My continental colleagues all say that the single most important British contribution to English studies is practical criticism, and that literary discussion is both a sensible focus for an orientation to the national past and an educational pursuit that engages students in a deeply personal way—an obvious candidate for one-to-one tutorials. The kinds of published scholarship growing out of this tradition, moreover, have always been extremely valuable in sensitising foreign students to English literature—to the systems of values and conventions of writing and reading it assumes. Obviously such work must be sustained and further developed. Perhaps even more attention will be paid to philosophical questions about the nature and goals of literary scholarship, and American literature, Commonwealth literature and world literature in English may also be given more house-room. Great strides have been taken in the past decade or so, but continental observers still think that British literary scholarship is somewhat unselfconscious and introverted.

Certainly, a few British literary scholars still behave with a closed-shop arrogance which foreigners can be excused for finding quaint, not least because it never had a continental counterpart. Both in Britain and elsewhere, classical studies were long regarded as a civilising and prestigious education, and the study of vernacular literature did not really get under way until the nineteenth century. But there the common history comes to an end. In Britain, literary intellectuals from Arnold onwards tended to suggest that English literature could even remedy modern man's spiritual emptiness and confusion, and the new type of literary education also laid some claim to the classics' old aura of gentility. Leavis, though often thought of as a unique force, merely brought these attitudes more fully into the open, and his idea was that English literature could be the central university subject, the ideal educational focus for an élite to be entrusted with power and influence: its students would become a Coleridgean clerisy who would guide society towards the true life. With the waning of the classics on the continent, however, higher education in science, technology and economics came to hold a much higher place than they did in Britain and training for the top positions was more vocational. Continental students of the national literatures regard themselves as keeping alive a heritage, but would hardly make more grandiose claims, and continental English scholars are puzzled by Leavis's apparent conviction that he belonged to a minority of the truly human, and by the scorn he sometimes poured on other people. C. P. Snow, if one of his aims was to remove the chip from the shoulders of British engineers, was merely being sensible.

Still, even in Britain most people would probably accept this now. Marxist critics, indeed, may tend to discredit Leavis too roundly, as if he had had no social engagement at all. At a time when American New Critics were labelling as fallacies statements about what real writers and real readers think and feel, quite consistently refraining from value judgements or any suggestions as to an American canon, Leavis proclaimed an indistinguishability of literary and moral values and offered for inspection his 'line' and his 'tradition'.

Continental scholars, so often taunted at home with being unable to 'popularise' their subject, have a grudging admiration for the public spiritedness with which Leavis and other British teachers, both in their university work and through journalism, have articulated a response to contemporary cultural phenomena. This outgoing dedication perhaps sorts rather oddly with some of the protestations of élitist cultural pessimism. Yet the new responsibility I have been heralding in British English departments may be little more than the transmogrification of a spirit that has been active all along. Despite the hereditary traces of closed-shop prickliness, most academic critics have gone on assuming that sharing their responses with others is both possible and worthwhile, so that in the era of Butler and Robbins practical criticism and literary evaluation, the clerisy's mystery, have percolated downwards to the common man. Millions of people nowadays could put up a better show than the writers of Richards's original protocols. Not that one should be too glib: I have already mentioned problems of cultural division and illiteracy; not even literacy is a guarantee against obtuseness; and what Leavis called mass civilisation still alarms. Yet his work did bear democratic fruit. The grammar-school boy who was intimidated on his first experience of Cambridge in the 1950s did learn the mind-style, and often went on to teach it, efficiently, in comprehensive or polytechnic, in new university or college of education.

Or abroad. As I say, the linguistic sensitivity of foreigners is very much a matter of the length and depth of their cultural immersion. In many cases, their response to English literature needs no apology. Whereas for the single-honours British student the English department is something of a finishing school—a short, decisive and often passionate stage in his acculturation within his own society—the continental English student, with the breadth and gradualness of his education, with his native-speaker knowledge of another language and its culture, with his lack of self-deception as to his grasp of English-language cultures past and present, is a different reader, but not a worse one. Some continental professors of English, particularly of the older generation, are intimidated by what remains of the British pride of sensibility, perhaps remembering the authority it seemed to carry when they were young. So they say that English literature is a more natural field of study for a British department, English language for a foreign. Younger colleagues, however, often see things differently. As language teachers in many ages and countries have realised, reading literary texts is the easiest and cheapest form of cultural immersion. English literature is also one of the main areas where continental departments could make more of the subject's humanistic potential, and some foreigners actually go on to make important contributions to English literary scholarship. Looking at things the other way round, moreover, English students in Britain would in no way be handicapped for citizenship by a more thorough understanding of their mother tongue. They are also in a rather convenient position to set about studying it, particularly if they know at least one other language and its culture as well, something which educationalists such as Christopher Brumfit now insist on as every Briton's right.

Modern linguistic approaches should be strongly represented in any English department, British or otherwise. Yet while there are linguists in Britain, many of them doing first-rate work on English, and some of them based in English departments—Lancaster, Nottingham, University College London, Edinburgh, Birmingham and East Anglia spring to mind—many others work in departments of linguistics, so that English departments are not in receipt of their findings in the most straightforward manner—Sheffield University's Department of English Language and Linguistics is institutionally unusual. The danger is that this may hold up developments on several fronts. For instance, I shall not detract from the achievements of British Old and Middle English philology if I observe that they have been at the cost of certain restrictions of scope. Phonology has been very strong, but syntax has been weaker. And what many continental colleagues would like to see is an increased British effort towards a historical text-linguistics, pragmatics, and sociolinguistics of English: the bottom-up approach, for example from the phoneme, needs to be complemented by top-down considerations. Such research, extending to the Englishes of all places and all periods, would necessarily investigate the forms and functions of English as the major world language, of which RP is merely one of the versions sometimes taught as models.

If there were a more solid grounding in linguistics, courses that combine linguistics with literary analysis and theory would lose their unwarranted air of contrivance. Much has changed over the past decade,[3] but a sense of conflict between language and literature has been part of the British frame of mind since at least the 1880s when Napier was appointed Merton Professor to the chagrin of Churton Collins.[4] This has also been the least fortunate of Britain's exports to English departments on the continent, but it should actually be seen in a far larger context as well: the relationship between linguistics and poetics has proved difficult in still other scholarly traditions. Looking back from the 1980s, we can see that one of the main weaknesses in attempts at an alignment of interests here, for the Russian Formalists no less than for British scholars, has been the premise, implicit or explicit, that language is the material from which literature is made. The next step has been to argue that literary categories are therefore predetermined by, and even coextensive with, hard-core linguistic categories. Taken to extremes, this resulted in those bottom-up analyses of literary texts which loaded every phoneme with definite artistic significance. Linguists could easily tire of it, since it involved little more than exhaustive descriptions. Literary scholars could easily feel that it represented a positivism blind to larger and more subtle organisations and effects, including some of those in which language did play a significant part.

I have hinted, however, that linguists are now developing a stylistics, a text-linguistics, a discourse analysis, a sociolinguistics, a pragmatics, which enable us to see entire processes of language production and reception as specific to particular sociocultural, situational and interactional circumstances. Furthermore, this emphasis by present-day linguists on contextualisation seems to be paralleled by certain hitherto quite separate developments in several kinds of literary scholarship. Sometimes within a Marxist framework, there is much discussion of how it is that literary texts, as the result of sociocultural forces, come to be designated as literary in the first place. American 'new' historians are exploring fascinating and unexpected aspects of the consubstantiality of literary texts with the cultures in which they are written and first read, and even the more traditional historical approach is renewing itself, not least by establishing closer links between the tasks of the bibliographer and those of the critic: the literary text's circumstances of publication are being brought into the very centre of the interpretative arena. Somewhat similarly, *Rezeptionsästhetik* has relativised the significance of literary works to the horizons of expectations of particular audiences, while German and Dutch empirical literary scientists are busily testing the responses of real readers in particular communities. Last but by no means least, the West's discovery of Bakhtin is leading to insights into relationships between the languages of literature and the vast range of sociolects—the heteroglossia—operative within any language community.

So the question is: Does contextualisation represent a real community of interest? Can it bring linguist and literary scholar on to speaking terms with each other? On the continent, but also in Britain, a growing number of people believe that it can. The promise of what they sometimes call literary pragmatics lies in its inclusion of a top-down perspective from the very start. Drawing on Enkvist's account of interpretability,[5] Bakhtin's sociological poetics, and Roger Fowler's account of literature as social discourse,[6] it sees the writing and reading of literary texts as interactive (albeit not face-to-face or one-to-one) communication processes, inextricably linked, like all such processes, with the particular sociocultural contexts in which they take place. It assumes that no account of communication in general will be complete without an explanation of literature and its contextualisation, and that no account of literature will be complete without an explanation of its employment of the communicative resources generally available. In effect, it reinstates the ancient connection between poetics and rhetoric and does so in a way that could well be of lasting importance for language scholars and literary scholars alike. Strict demarcations between the two callings begin to seem questionable.

Generally speaking, connections between what are still often seen as distinct subject areas stand a very fair chance of success in Britain. Much of the credit for the favourable climate must go to the new universities, one of whose aims was precisely to move away from the single-subject honours degree towards a genuine interdisciplinarity.[7] British higher education now offers some interesting area studies approaches to the United States, and some English departments, particularly in the polytechnics, are following leads given by Richard Hoggart and Raymond Williams in the study of culture, communications, and the relationship between literature and history.[8] Such trends should also be seen against both the current de-specialisation of the sixth form and the still influential precedents set within older institutions. At Oxford, it was by stressing the literature-history relationship that Helen Gardner resisted New Criticism, and much the same was true of Leavis and L. C. Knights at Cambridge.[9] Cambridge, indeed, always balanced practical criticism with 'life and thought', and the saddest thing about Basil Willey's work was simply his use of the word 'background' in his titles: it may have encouraged people to think that literature is either more or less important than, and not really a part of, everything else.

Some continental scholars are themselves participating in new interdisciplinary ventures. In Copenhagen much teaching and research in English has moved out of the English department into the School of Economics, the Centre for Mediaeval Studies, the Centre for Women's Studies, the Centre for Translation, and so on. The Danes seem satisfied with this arrangement—it has brought them better funding—and they are beginning to say that the idea of the separate language department is archaic. Probably their interdisciplinary centres are generating more meaningful synergy than the vast array of options in German and Swiss English departments, where little is officially done to suggest the bearing of one thing on another, and students often feel lost. But the problem is obviously to avoid a false or premature synthesis—such as may sometimes be attempted within Marxist and feminist frameworks, in Britain and elsewhere—or a level of generality too high for precise and significant scholarship.

The British, who abroad are still stereotyped as empirical, are generally not expected to fall into these traps. Nor would the suggestion be that they emulate Masson's six-volume-plus-index *The Life of John Milton, Narrated in Connexion with the Political, Ecclesiastical, and Literary History of His Time*, important though such great works remain. There are, rather, the new insights now, of pragmatics and literary pragmatics, and the study of history and culture would naturally fall in with these. Whereas continental departments have often stressed 'civilisation', some British departments are still so fixed in the reaction against the comparative philology and biographical criticism of the age of Masson, so specialised to *langue*, to the forms of utterances, to texts, that the sociocultural and *realia* contexts of English in its various uses, literary and other, receive too little attention. This again amounts to an unawareness of the pragmatic interdependence, in the generation of all meaning and interactive force, of linguistic code and context of use. Its effects will only be aggravated in a department where literary theory is still at the stage of deconstruction.[10] British undergraduates are sometimes launched on to seas of semiosis that are unnecessarily quirky, though some British scholars have long recognised the need for explanatory notes in editions of classical English novels,[11] and this may eventually draw attention to the larger problem.

What I have been saying, then, is that to people on the continent British higher education seems very exotic, but that there is much in the British educational experience, and in British English studies, which continental English scholars can only admire. By following the British example, continental departments could do more to release the potential of their students, particularly in matters of proficiency training and literary analysis. At the same time, British departments, while opening up and giving greater intellectual rigour to their tradition of literary studies, could also become still more responsible about language in society at large, more committed to linguistic approaches in general, and still more ready to pursue interdisciplinary connections, especially those between language and literature and society. Without endangering the rich variety resulting from British traditions of local autonomy in matters educational, English as a subject could in fact become slightly more the same in the whole of Europe, and there is nothing in the difference between native speaker and foreigner to prevent this. Here is one area in which the 1992 miracle could profitably come to pass.

*Notes*

[1] I actually sent out a steeplechase of a questionnaire. The following colleagues stood the course and I am deeply in their debt: Prof. Balz Engler (Basle); Prof. Waldemar Zacharasiewicz (Vienna); Prof. F. K. Stanzel (Graz); Prof. J. P. Vander Motten (Ghent); Prof. Alan E. Boucher (Iceland); Prof. Arne Zettersten and Dr Graham Caie (Copenhagen); Prof. Bernd Dietz · (Universidad de La Laguna, Teneriffe); Dr Willie Van Peer (Utrecht); Dr Peter Verdonk (University of Amsterdam); Dr Gerard Steen (Free University

of Amsterdam); Dr Keith Batterbee (Turku); Prof. Matti Rissanen (Helsinki); Prof. Kari Sajavaara (Jyväsklylä); Prof. Nils Erik Enkvist (Åbo Akademi); Prof. Kay Wikberg (Oslo); Prof. Jeremy Hawthorn (Trondheim); Prof. Claes Schaar (Lund); Prof. Willis Edmonson (Hamburg); Prof. Herbert Grabes (Giessen); Dr Anna Torti (Verona).

2 Judging, for instance, by Sidney Greenbaum, *Good English and the Grammarian*, Longman: London, 1988.

3 See Ronald Carter in the present volume.

4 See D. J. Palmer, *The Rise of English Studies*, Oxford University Press: London, 1965, pp. 78–103.

5. Nils Erik Enkvist, 'On the Interpretability of Texts in General and of Literary Texts in Particular,' in Roger D. Sell (ed.), *Literary Pragmatics: Proceedings of the 1988 Åbo Symposium* (forthcoming).

6 Roger Fowler, *Literature as Social Discourse*, Batsford: London, 1981.

7 Cf. Palmer, p. 161, and Michael Irwin in the present volume.

8 Cf. Raymond Cowell (Dean of the Faculty of Humanities at the Sunderland Polytechnic), *The Critical Enterprise: English Studies in Higher Education*, Allen & Unwin: London, 1975, esp. pp. 64–74. See also Michael Green, 'The Centre for Contemporary Cultural Studies', in Peter Widdowson (ed.) *Re-Reading English*, Methuen: London, 1982, pp. 77–90.

9 Helen Gardner, *The Business of Criticism*, Oxford University Press: London, 1959, esp. pp 25–51; F. R. Leavis, *Education and the University: A Sketch for and 'English School'*, Chatto & Windus: London, 1943, new edn 1948, pp. 63–64; L. C. Knights, 'The University Teaching of English and History', in his *Explorations*, 1946; Penguin: Harmondsworth, 1964, pp. 191–203.

10 See Roger D. Sell, 'Grammatology and Literary Pragmatics' (The 1988 PALA Lecture: The Poetics and Linguistics Association, forthcoming).

11 Cf. Stephen Wall, 'Annotated English Novels?' *Essays in Criticism XXXII (1982)* 1–8.

# Notes on editor and contributors

Martin Dodsworth is Professor of English at Royal Holloway and Bedford New College in the University of London. He is chairman of the English Association and also of the Committee for University English which was formed in 1988. For some time he edited the English Association's journal, *English*; he is the author of *Hamlet Closely Observed* (1986).

Isobel Armstrong, formerly Professor of English at the University of Southampton, and now Professor of English at Birkbeck College, University of London, has written extensively on nineteenth-century English poetry. She has just completed the Victorian volume of *The Routledge History of English Poetry*.

Lyn Pykett is a lecturer in English at the University College of Wales, Aberystwyth, but has also taught O-and A-level English in Colleges of Further Education. She has published a number of articles on nineteenth-and twentieth-century fiction and on the Victorian periodical press. A book on Emily Brontë is to be published in 1989.

Peter Corbin has been Head of the School of English in the University of Exeter, where he is a Senior Lecturer, since 1980. His main research interests are in Renaissance and modern drama. He has recently published *Three Jacobean Witchcraft Plays* (1986) and *An Annotated Critical Bibliography of Jacobean and Caroline Comedy* (1988), both with Douglas Sedge.

Ronald Carter is Senior Lecturer in English Studies and Director of the Centre for English Language Education at the University of Nottingham. He has published widely in the field of linguistics, literature and education; his books include *Language and Literature: A Reader in Stylistics* (1982) and *Literature and Language Teaching* (1986), which he edited with C. J. Brumfit.

Michael Irwin is Professor of English at the University of Kent, and author of *Picturing: Description and Illusion in the Nineteenth-Century Novel* (1979).

Daniel Lamont is head of the School of Language and Literature at Lancashire Polytechnic and Treasurer to the Standing Conference on English in Public Sector Higher Education. He has a particular interest in inter-disciplinary teaching.

Roger D. Sell is Professor of English Language and Literature at Åbo Akademi, Finland. He has published on a wide range of English literature from Chaucer to the twentieth century and is leader of the Literary Pragmatics Project of the Academy of Finland.

———